Coaching Champions

HOW TO BUILD A WINNING SALES TEAM

SECOND EDITION

Frank Salisbury

Published by
OAK TREE PRESS
19 Rutland Street, Cork, Ireland
www.oaktreepress.com

© 2011 Frank Salisbury

Frank Salisbury has asserted his right to be
identified as the author of this work.

A catalogue record of this book is
available from the British Library.

ISBN 978 1 904887 65 2 (Paperback)
ISBN 978 1 904887 66 9 (PDF)
ISBN 978 1 904887 67 6 (ePub)
ISBN 978 1 904887 68 3 (Kindle)

CONTENTS

FIGURES

ACKNOWLEDGEMENTS

I would like to acknowledge the contributions made by Cariona Neary and Karl O'Connor to the first edition of this book (*Coaching Champions: How to Get the Best Out of Your Salespeople*).

In particular, I thank Sandy Metcalfe and my other colleagues in Business & Training Solutions International, who have applied the lessons from this book into the real world of business and sales, with remarkable success.

As always, I am indebted to Pauline, who continues to endure my obsession with this topic, as well as correcting my poor spelling.

PREFACE

Sales management success is as difficult to understand as life itself. People are complicated and their personalities are complex. If anyone tells you that they have the secret of success in sales management, smell their breath.

It could be just that I am getting older. However, I would like to think that age has brought with it a certain amount of valuable and relevant experience but that I have not become the sort of person who used to annoy me by saying "it wasn't like this in my day". I have to say, though, it *wasn't* like this in my day. Sales management, that is.

Why talk of sales management, when this book is about sales coaching? It's because I believe that, if you acquire the knowledge and learn the skills laid out in this book, you might not have to manage people – they just might let you coach them. None of us like being managed – and that includes your sales team. Sometimes, we forget what it was like to be a salesperson. Perhaps this book will help you to remember and to avoid all of the things you promised you would not do before you became a sales manager.

A great disappointment to me is that there are too many sales managers, and far too many companies, who believe that selling and/ or sales management can be learned in two days. This does not stop companies from running two-day sales courses and expecting people to perform instantly thereafter. Only the other day, I was discussing with a senior training manager the sales training needs he had. When he started with "I'm always interested in seeing new techniques and processes", I knew I was in trouble. At that stage, I ignored the first rule of my own training and told him what I thought, which was not what he wanted hear – namely, that the answer to sales success lies within the behaviour of those who are already successful in the company, not with him or me.

My problem is that I am becoming increasingly intolerant of amateurs. Perhaps it is a function of age. It is also, I suppose, a function of confidence in my own ability and the success that it has brought. I do not need to deal with people who do not want to deal with me. I recall a successful colleague of mine who said to me, a great many years ago, "I do not sell to people who do not want to buy from me. Therefore I assume, before I visit anybody, that they all want to buy from me". I agree with the sentiment and, having adopted that sort of attitude on many occasions, have found it most successful.

People like dealing with confident people and, in selling, sometimes the more you give the impression that you are not going to take it personally if they do not buy, the more it seems to attract people. In the case of the potential customer I was talking to, I was too bothered. I tried to teach him in five minutes, which was the level of attention he gave to the subject, what had taken me a lifetime to learn. I should have walked away there and then. It did me no emotional favours trying to sell him something he simply could not understand, and this is something worth learning for everyone considering a professional career in selling.

What I learned a long time ago, and it's worth keeping in mind yourself, is that sustainable sales success has less to do with the sales team than it has to do with the person managing the sales team. Not only are you key to sales success but you are also accountable for sales failure. I say accountable rather than responsible – something which will be explained in more detail later in the book.

I cannot force you to read and act upon the material contained in this book, but if you are looking for the answer to sales success in some miracle technique or phrase, then you may be disappointed. As I told the training manager, the answer to sales success lies within. However, he did not believe me either.

It may not be in fashion these days but, for most, if not all, of this book, I have attempted to keep it simple. Whenever I am asked to help companies to analyse their sales training needs, I do not approach the task as though it was a precursor to writing a paper on nuclear fusion. To me, sales training is a simple matter of deciding what the company wants to say to the customer and teaching the sales team:

- To consistently say it.
- To consistently say it better.
- To sound and look convincing whilst they are saying it.

I truly believe that, if you get any more complicated than this, you might have lost the plot.

In some of the material, I talk about the 'professional game of selling'. I have spent a lot of time over the last few years comparing sports with selling. Like many people in selling, I have attended sales conferences and seminars where sporting analogies and images were used to elicit some motivation amongst the audience. In common with most in the audience and all those presenting, I was unable to apply those analogies in the 'real world', as salespeople and managers are liable to call it. Few of us can recall pole-vaulting into the office, and the last time we did 100 metres in less than 10 seconds was when the boss came a-calling.

Yet when I really began to understand how athletes become professional, I realised that the truth was staring me in the face all the time. In addition, the same evidence exists in the professions of acting, dancing and music. Hopefully, this will be as much of a revelation to you as it was to me.

It is within this premise that I set out my stall deliberately to challenge you to question everything you have ever known or held dear about selling, sales management and professionalism. I think that selling is an honourable profession practised by many amateurs. It is about time that we realised that selling is a physical skill, which requires salespeople, sales managers, and sales trainers alike to apply the simple processes of repetition and hard work, in order to have a successful outcome.

This book does not contain the answers to sales management success. It merely contains the background reading material. Having said that, contrary to popular belief, selling is a well-researched and well-recorded activity and the bookshops and libraries are full of books, articles, and research papers covering every aspect of selling. You just need to know where to look.

The book should be viewed as part of a process of self-discovery. It is through self-awareness of who we are, what we want to be, and what the barriers are to our potential success that we can begin to tackle those barriers in order to achieve the potential that lies within us all.

Lastly, if there is one thing you can apply very quickly and which will stand you in good stead in your working life, it is 'treat other people as you would want to be treated yourself'. Apply this principle each day, and you will not go far wrong.

This book is the culmination of over 30 years' research into what makes sales teams successful. I hope it helps you to avoid some of the pain it took me to learn some of these hard lessons.

Frank Salisbury
Joint Founder, Institute of Professional Selling
May 2011
Dublin

CHAPTER 1
THE SEEDS OF GREATNESS

No one's so good, they cannot get better. *Nick Faldo*

THE CHALLENGE

Nick Faldo's comment on the world of golf can be applied equally in the business world. It's a statement that must have a special resonance for sales managers as they face year after year of ever-tougher targets. How can you continue to improve? And how can you get your top performers to do even better, reach even higher targets? Sales managers face enormous challenges in harnessing their team and driving them towards a goal of continuous improvement. Indeed, one of the greatest issues today is to recruit and retain good salespeople. Top performers who do not feel challenged or acknowledged vote with their feet in markets where their skills and talents are in strong demand.

We all come to work with an existing level of knowledge, skills and attitudes. Training releases a further level but, for most people, a significant mass of knowledge, skills and the attitudes that lead to successful performance remains untapped. Denis Waitley calls it the seed of greatness.[1] I call it the Performance Potential Iceberg (**Figure 1**). Whatever you call it, the premise is the same: we all have talents and skills that are unrealised.

All the evidence points to one fact: the sales manager can make the difference between the performance of a good sales team and that of an outstanding sales team. Exit interviews conducted in many organisations before people leave their employers have highlighted that salespeople do not leave jobs because they were unhappy with the company; they leave because they were unhappy with their

---

[1] Denis Waitley, *Seeds of Greatness,* Simon and Schuster, 1983.

manager. But this is a two-sided coin. If you have the skills to lead, motivate, challenge and share your vision with your team, then you are on the road to higher productivity, higher profitability and higher customer satisfaction, as well as higher staff retention.

So, is it easy? No: it takes a fundamental shift in the way you lead your team. It is about taking a journey, starting with yourself and your own barriers to greater performance. For some people, it is a long and sometimes winding road that leads them to embrace the concept of coaching.

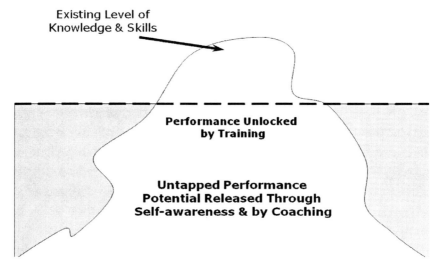

Figure 1: The Performance Potential Iceberg

Just as our sales team is made up of individuals whose full potential is as yet untapped, the same is true of sales managers. We ourselves must learn the core skills of coaching: questioning, listening, observing, and providing feedback. We need to examine our attitudes towards people's potential and we need to learn how to develop a new foundation for our relationship with our sales team. Such a relationship must be based on the salesperson taking responsibility for their own performance, on increased self-awareness of the salesperson and on trust and belief rather than blame and recrimination.

FROM SPORTS COACH TO SALES MANAGEMENT COACH

Do you need to hold an Olympic gold medal in long-distance running to be able to coach an aspiring marathon runner? Do you need to have a bagful of football caps to be able to coach the national football team? In the sports world, great coaches must be just that: great coaches. We do not expect them to have achieved all the goals they set for the sportspeople they are coaching. Yet in business, we believe the most effective sales managers and coaches should have a track record as successful salespeople. Why?

Whilst many of us have had the misfortune of meeting mediocre trainers who lacked the requisite job knowledge and application, the experience of working on the coaching model in this book has thrown into significant doubt the theory that you first must be a practitioner before you become a trainer. In the years since I first developed the POWER© coaching model, I have coached people to play better snooker and golf — even though my own skills in both leave a lot to be desired! There are many examples of leaders from the worlds of the creative arts and sports improving the skills of business managers using coaching techniques, without themselves having been in management. Granted, coaches need knowledge of the job to be done, but they need to be neither proficient nor expert in the role being coached. However, the person being coached must have a basic knowledge or understanding of the skill before coaching can commence.

Coaching is a development tool that can only be productive after skills training has taken place. A salesperson who has just been appointed to the job cannot be coached to achieve 'stretch' targets without some basic training being provided in the first instance – for example, in product knowledge. While trainers, in most cases, need to have first-hand experience of the job, those coaching require different attributes and skills.

As in sports, coaching in business is about winning. The sales manager is responsible for winning, for keeping his/her salespeople focused on goals, for nurturing their self-belief and for motivating them to become champions in their field.

SALES COACHING: A DEFINITION

In my book *Developing Managers as Coaches*,[2] I defined coaching as:

> The release of latent talent and skills, previously untapped by training, through a process of self-awareness initiated by the coach.

More recently, I have updated that definition to produce a definition exclusive to sales coaching:

> A process whereby the sales coach enables a salesperson to focus on the elements of their performance that either directly contribute to or hinder their sales success and assists in the construction and implementation of plans of action in order to ensure continuous improvement.

TRAINERS AND MANAGERS

If you accept that the sales manager is a key influence on the performance of the sales team, then where does that leave training? Sales managers often blame the training function for their team's underperformance. Yet I am convinced that the reason training fails to deliver is due primarily to line management's apathy and the lack of support for field training activities. However, line management is not solely responsible for this situation. The problem is exacerbated by the trainer's inability to show the manager any real lasting benefit from training. Trainers and managers are as far apart from each other these days as they have ever been, each blaming the other for performance shortfalls in trainees. From the two seemingly opposing camps, I often hear remarks such as the following:

- **Managers:** "If those people in training only came down from their ivory towers and tried dealing with reality, it might do them a world of good".

---

[2]   Frank Salisbury, *Developing Managers as Coaches: A Trainer's Guide*, McGraw-Hill, 1996.

- **Trainers:** "What's the point of training anybody simply to send them into the clutches of a management team oblivious to the needs of continuous training?".

Neither attitude is helpful, either to the relationship between trainers and managers or to the organisation and the rest of the people working in it.

What coaching has done for me — and it can do the same for you — is to bring managers and trainers together, focusing on a common goal, using the same ball, and playing as a team on a level playing field. By using a common philosophy and language, I have observed a change in the manager/trainer relationship that produces in each a trust in the skills that each player has and the desire of each to excel and to have their charges excel – the premise being that each person can excel at a job, given the opportunity and assistance to do so.

In terms of the skills we have and can acquire, at the moment of birth we are all equal. We have our parents' genes, but external factors being equal, we all have the same opportunity for greatness. Those external factors, such as family and schooling, soon play a major role in influencing our journey and eventual destination.

These and other similar self-evident truths aside, it is clear that managers, computer programmers, doctors, lawyers, clerks, drivers, salespeople, and a thousand other job-holders, whether classified as professionals or not, are not born to those professions, but are fabricated into them by their environment and chance. Correspondingly, neither these nor the unemployed and the unemployable are products of genetic certainty, but of circumstance, opportunity and, most importantly, the loving care and attention given to their seeds of greatness – or perhaps the lack of it. As George Eliot put it: "It is never too late to be what you might have been".

Everyone has it within themselves to deliver personal performances of excellence beyond their currently perceived limits of aspiration. My contention, supported by my own experience and practical research into sales management, is that people at work have greater aspirations than either their manager realises, or than those they are willing to share with their manager. I propose that the manager who operates as a coach can bring the seed of greatness to the surface in all its glory. I am not inviting managers to lead from behind, but to rid themselves of the normal managerial trait of telling. By adopting the principles espoused in this book, they can reap the harvest of the seeds of greatness within their sales teams.

THE 'TELLING' TRAP

It may seem a simple piece of advice to put into action, but, in my experience, one of the greatest challenges for managers in adopting the principles of coaching is to give up telling other people what to do — when appropriate. Managers seem to find it difficult to know when it is not appropriate. Phrases like "She's a natural leader", "He takes charge immediately", "They lead from the front" and so on advocate that leading and managing is about telling people what to do. It's a natural enough phenomenon. We grow up being told what to do by our parents; it is something we expect. It is hardly surprising, therefore, that as parents we then fall into the 'telling' trap ourselves. Many may argue that this is necessary. What is certainly neither necessary nor desirable is that, when we become managers, we tend constantly to tell others what to do. Certainly, there are occasions when telling is required. A new employee needs to be told and shown, what to do on the job and how to do it. Coaching someone through an emergency is not appropriate and, although it may result in empowerment of the individual, it might also lead to tears and injury.

The educational system, from primary to secondary school, continues the process of telling begun by our parents and, for the vast majority of people, entry into the labour market exposes us to yet more instructions. Those leaving secondary school and entering the more liberal environment of colleges and universities experience self-directed learning for the first time, where students must take responsibility for their own education. However, the patterns of interaction in a learning environment set down in those early years are a form of mental programming that is difficult to change in later life. Newly-appointed managers often do not receive appropriate formal training in their new role, so they slip back into the old habits of telling, which implies "I know best, so let me do the thinking". Can we really expect outstanding performance from people who do not even get a chance to shape their own goals?

COACHING IS NOT COUNSELLING

Many managers confuse coaching with being soft, showing weakness when what is required is strength. Coaching is not a soft option. It requires strength of character. It requires managers to be strong in their belief that people have the solution to their performance problems within them. It requires that managers have the courage to let go.

Coaching also is confused with counselling. It can be similar, but it is not the same. The British Association for Counselling defines counselling as:

> The skilled and principled use of the relationship to facilitate self-knowledge, emotional acceptance and growth, and the optimal development of personal resources.

In coaching, as in counselling, the answer to performance problems and potential lies within each individual and, as with counselling, those answers can be extracted by careful and systematic questioning. To that end, sales coaching also seeks to bring about self-awareness in the. In coaching roles within organisations, however, the coach has a clear objective to focus people on performance issues. The coach has a goal, and that goal is almost always tied in with organisational objectives. Managers as coaches also have an additional responsibility and accountability and, therefore, are concerned additionally with timescales. The seed of greatness has to be tended and nurtured, but it also has to provide and deliver.

Coaches are not counsellors. The difference between coaching and counselling is that coaching focuses on individual and, ultimately, organisational performance, while counselling is focused on the individual alone. As a sales coach, you have a responsibility to move salespeople forward towards a corporate aim. That movement forward involves wasted expense in, for example, management and salesperson time if results are not being achieved. The company coach, therefore, is acutely aware of when to pull the plug if results are not being achieved, following this mutual investment in time through the application of the coaching model I present in this book. A counsellor does not have that responsibility: they may have the desire to move people forward, but the responsibility for the timescale rests with the individual.

Counselling is focused on helping the individual to overcome problems encountered, while coaching is geared towards developing the performer to realise future opportunities.

CONCEPT, PRACTICE, PROCESS

This book is about a new way of developing, managing and empowering people. It is about adopting coaching as a concept, a practice and a process. It is a way of thinking that should be embodied within your own beliefs about people and their untapped abilities. The concept holds that most people want to contribute more than they currently are allowed to, that they want to belong and to be in control of their own destinies, but that, somewhere along the journey, they were hijacked. The practice requires transference from the theory of the classroom to the reality of work. It requires managers to release people from the chains of telling and of rules and regulations and conformity. It requires managers to understand that subordinates have the same feelings of responsibility as they do, and that trust is something to be shared — it is a two-way process. But trusting is a risky business which takes time to build — "I tried that once and it did not work!". So try it again until it does.

ANYONE CAN BE A COACH!

This book is written specifically for people in sales and sales management. Whether as coach or as someone being coached, there should be something here for you. Anyone can be a coach, in any situation, providing there exists a genuine desire to adopt these coaching principles. There also needs to be a shared vision, trust, and mutual support. Furthermore, coaches need to believe in the premise that all people can grow. The coach has to have a clear vision of that growth, both for themselves and the people they work with. The greatest gift a coach can give is time — time to coach.

In this book, I explore the need for managers as coaches to be aware of the levels of competence in their salespeople as they acquire new skills and insights, moving from a state of unconscious incompetence through to unconscious competence in selling. It is like learning to ride a bike. In the first stage, the person is unaware that they cannot cycle, while at the unconscious competence stage, they cycle without thinking about the skills they have learned through trial and error.

This book focuses on the POWER© coaching model, whose name is an acronym for:

- Purpose.
- Objectives and Options.
- What is happening now?
- Empowering.
- Review.

Using the techniques suggested, sales managers and salespeople will be able to increase the successes they have with their teams. To stop learning is to stop living. The most important thing we can do as managers is to encourage others to keep learning. To do that, managers and coaches must lead by example. The worst anyone can do is to assume they have heard it all before. Yet the most common barrier to increased ability is usually the existence of restricted vision and a closed mind. Coaching is not another one-year-only panacea. A major problem with many development programmes is that they are constantly shifting direction, depending on the whims of the incumbent chief executive or the training/HR manager. Coaching is an integral part of a whole development programme — but, for a change, one that works.

However, if you want coaching to work, then you also must decide that you will stick with it until you and your team get it right. Coaching challenges you to change the habits of a lifetime, to adopt new concepts, new ways of dealing with old situations. It can take years, rather than weeks or months, to embed itself properly. Is that a bad thing? A long-term approach to coaching displays to the troops your commitment to making something work. That philosophy, unfortunately, does not fit well with Western business culture. We tend to work to shorter timescales. Some companies cannot see further than the quarter-end figures, and then they wonder why no real planning takes place. It is important that everybody in the company understands the longevity of your coaching plans and philosophy.

The seed of greatness exists for all those who say they can, and even within those who say they cannot. Coaching can release that seed, not just for the person being coached, but also for the coach. This book can change your performance for the better. It represents for me a model upon which personal performance issues are clearly defined, structured and acted upon. It can do the same for you and for the people you seek to develop. It is the missing piece of the people development jigsaw. Coaching offers a roadmap in the long journey to discover a better way of managing, training and developing salespeople.

CHAPTER 2
SALESPEOPLE

Everything in life is selling. *Robert Louis Stevenson*

LOOKING FOR THE NATURAL-BORN SALES WONDER

If we are to explore what sales coaching is, then we must also explore what selling is and who you will be coaching. It is every sales manager's dream to have a team of top salespeople, but born salespeople seem very hard to find. How can you identify and attract successful salespeople to your company? How can you keep them happy? Is there such a thing as the 'natural-born sales wonder' in your business and, if so, what are his or her attributes?

There are a number of chosen professions that may rely heavily on a particular physical attribute of some form or another but can we honestly believe that, before birth, some people are destined to be doctors, accountants, musicians, footballers, lawyers, actors, traffic wardens, managers, or salespeople? If this were the case, then Eric Clapton and Madonna could have been born in the middle of a Brazilian jungle but still played to packed audiences in the local hut; Cristiano Ronaldo could have been born in an igloo in Alaska but would be the highest paid footballer in the Alaska Premier division. It's about as unlikely as being born a salesperson.

WHAT MAKES A SUCCESSFUL SALESPERSON?

I have been researching the area of successful attributes for many years to see whether there are any distinctive personality traits or demographic profiles that predispose certain individuals to be successful in selling. Clearly, many companies believe that the 'natural-born sales wonder' exists. Why else are huge resources put into administering and interpreting personality questionnaires in the recruitment and selection process? My research set about testing whether there were natural attributes that were consistently associated with success.

Starting with the most obvious traits, ones that can be ascertained from a CV, my research examined a number of demographic factors in salespeople — successful and unsuccessful ones — to see whether there were any factors relating to gender, age or education that consistently pointed to success or failure.

Gender

My research[3] found that, while men and women fail and succeed in equal percentages, women tend to be clustered at the top and bottom end of many salesforces, leading to a belief that they either succeed or fail dramatically. Most men, it seems, occupy the middle ground, with a few being highly successful. There are obviously exceptions, notably in financial services, where the vast majority of salespeople who fail are men — mainly due to the fact that financial services direct salesforces are predominantly male. In many financial services companies, as many as 80 per cent of salespeople are not achieving target at any one time, and labour turnover runs on average at 60 per cent. Even in non-financial sales forces, some 55 per cent of people are not achieving target and labour turnover runs at around 40 per cent.

Age

Age appears to be insignificant: successful salespeople can be found across all age groups. The only determining factor about age with salespeople is that the older they are, the less they are willing to change, but then this attitude is not exclusive to sales. They can change. They can learn new skills. They choose not to.

Education

Whether salespeople hold qualifications appears to make little or no difference to their sales success. They may be assessed as being more competent than those without qualifications, but the effect that

3   Frank Salisbury, *The Effectiveness of Sales Training*, MPhil research, Oxford Brookes University, 1990.

competence has on sales success is not proven. The only way in which qualifications can enhance success in sales is in the confidence that it can give to the salesperson. Unfortunately, too many salespeople with qualifications believe that the customer should be impressed by their qualifications. They are not.

Experience and a Successful Track Record

According to my research, sales experience is not a strong indicator of future sales success. Experienced salespeople fail or succeed in equal numbers. This suggests that companies are unwise to place too strong an emphasis on experience in a recruitment drive. It certainly helps if a candidate has in-depth industry knowledge or is already familiar with the customer base, but it does not guarantee them sales success. In fact, trainees with no sales experience generally fare better than experienced salespeople in the short term. It is not so much that 'you cannot teach an old dog new tricks'; it's just that the old dog does not want to learn any new tricks.

Success does not transfer well from one company to another. A person who is successful in one company may not be able to repeat that success in a new environment. The flipside of this is that failing in one company does not mean that the salesperson will fail in a different company. Indeed, I found that the experience of failure, for both salespeople and for sales managers, was usually a spur to doing well in the future. Salespeople do have a tendency to learn from their mistakes and failures. Unfortunately for most companies, the salesperson usually applies that learning elsewhere.

Personality

Guion[4] has said that not only do sales roles differ but the personality characteristics required also vary greatly. This area of personality and recruitment is fraught with difficulties. Although a whole industry has grown up over the last 20 years supporting the theory that there is such a thing as a sales personality, I have grave doubts about the validity of the claims being made. Indeed, the scales of available research literature weigh heavily in favour of nurture as opposed to

---

[4]   R.M. Guion, *Personnel Testing*, McGraw-Hill, Maidenhead, 1965.

nature.[5] In addition, I believe that placing the onus on salespeople to have a particular personality somehow releases managers from the accountability of developing salespeople. People often use the word 'personality' on its own when what they really mean is a pleasing personality or a positive attitude. We all have a personality, for better or worse!

NO IDENTIKIT – ONLY BEHAVIOURAL CLUES

It is clear from the available research that it is not possible to seek out specific 'winner' personality characteristics or demographic profiles. My findings indicate very strongly that there is no such thing as a successful salesperson identikit. This does not seem very helpful to the sales manager who is under pressure to put together a high-performing team. However, there are certain behaviours that can be associated consistently with successful people, just as there are negative behaviours that are found among unsuccessful people.

For me, an exploration of the behaviours displayed by salespeople has turned out to reveal more about success and failure than either personality or demographic features. The research revealed a stark contrast between successful and unsuccessful salespeople.

Successful salespeople:

- Displayed more energy.
- Showed more initiative in finding business.
- Displayed more confidence in their own ability.
- Appeared to believe in what they were selling.
- Were fiercely loyal towards the company.
- Had a purpose in life and set clear goals with deadlines for achievement.

Yet most importantly, and this is consistent among all top performers in all professions, they accepted personal responsibility for their success and for any failures.

In addition, I found that successful salespeople displayed more:

---

5   David Shenk, *The Genius in All of Us*, Icon Books, 2010.

- Self-knowledge.
- Knowledge of product benefits.
- Knowledge of internal contacts who could help them.
- Desire to be in selling.
- Respect for the customer.

An important factor that separates top-performing salespeople from the rest is their attitude towards the customer. They know that they will continue to be successful only by helping other people get what they want. Successful salespeople:

- Are customer-focused rather than sales-focused.
- Employ low-pressure sales processes rather than high-pressure selling techniques.
- Understand the difference between 'I win and you win' and 'I win and you lose'.
- Would rather say 'the customer bought' than 'I sold'.

In addition — strange to say — top performers are also insecure. Seemingly, most do not know why they are performing at a high level, apart from hard work, and they are worried that whatever it is they have may one day be lost.

Nothing new, you might say. Yet my research also found that those who were failing were the type who:

- Instead of accepting responsibility for finding business, waited for the company to provide them with leads.
- Constantly made excuses about their performance, blaming it on the recession, the product, the organisation or their manager.
- Hid from contact with the manager and their peer group.
- Displayed a negative attitude towards the company.

You might hold the view that these salespeople were like this because of their failure, not that these behaviours caused their failure. The argument is not relevant. Once in the trap, few rarely emerge. What you have here, though, are two sets of behaviours that can be used to create a greater level of self-awareness regarding your own behaviour and that of your salespeople. As a sales coach, you need to support and encourage positive behaviours and help to change negative ones.

KNOWLEDGE

Knowledge, it is said, forms the basis of a salesperson's career. Without knowledge of the company's products, the market available, and the role of the company in that market, a salesperson may be placed at a disadvantage by customers' questions about the product, a situation that ultimately could result in missed sales opportunities.

Salespeople need product knowledge to give them additional confidence and, the more they know, the more confident they should be. High levels of product knowledge, however, like high academic qualifications, are no guarantee of sales success. Those with qualifications and/or high competency levels in terms of product knowledge are no more or less successful than those without.

There is a paradox about product knowledge. A salesperson should be an expert, but you have no need to prove to the customer that you are an expert by confusing them, or by droning on about your wealth of knowledge. The great French philosopher Voltaire once said that the best way to become boring is to say everything! Thus the maxim for the salesperson in terms of product knowledge must be: 'Know lots but talk little'. You cannot know too much about your products, but you can talk too much about them.

A high level of product knowledge may also make salespeople more confident, but confident about what? Many apparently confident salespeople fall to pieces in the face of a difficult customer or at the thought of cold telephoning. Their confidence is related to product knowledge and not to selling. In many organisations, more time is spent drumming knowledge into people rather than skills. To what end? If a company's product is dynamic and keeps changing, then knowledge has a short shelf-life, whereas skill can be on the increase always. If a salesperson were to spend as much time on skill acquisition as on knowledge accumulation, there would be a dramatic improvement in sales performance. It is far more important to find out what the product can become in the eyes of the customer than what it is.

SKILLS

Too many people believe that skills are acquired on a training course. All a training course ever can do is to make you aware of the need to learn a skill. The acquisition of a skill takes considerably longer than any company can afford to allow you to stay in a classroom (see **Figure 2**).

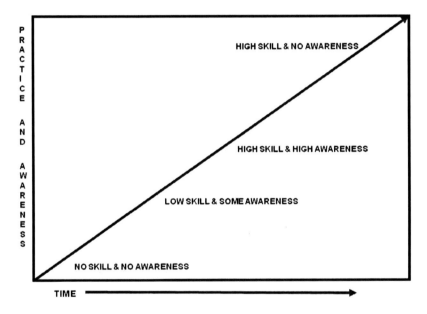

Figure 2: Skills Acquisition

Watching someone else sell can look deceptively easy, just as sitting next to someone who is skilled at driving is deceptive. It looks easy because they make it look easy. When you are sitting next to someone who is driving, you could be forgiven for saying to yourself, 'I could do that. It looks simple enough, and anyway, if they can do it, I'm sure I could too'. The same would be true of a sport such as snooker. It looks easy enough on television. When you first try and play it, however, you realise almost immediately how difficult it is.

The next step in the model is where you move to some awareness of your low skill. For example, suppose you try driving for the first time. For most of us, we will have been told how to start the car. Most of us will ignore the instruction completely and either stall the car or nearly burn the starter motor out in our keenness to show our level of competence, which at this stage is non-existent.

Driving, athletics, acting, music and dancing are all skills-based. You cannot learn these things from discussion, books or watching someone else do them. They are activities you have to experience, something you have to do. They are physical skills.

Selling is a physical skill. It cannot be learned from discussion; it is something you have to experience, something you have to 'do'. It is only through practising the skill that we can become aware of the potential length of the journey. Practice and failure makes us aware of where we are, like learning to drive. When you first get behind the wheel of the car, you realise how much there is to learn. The same principle should apply to selling. Yet in most cases, salespeople, sales managers and sales trainers fail to understand the analogy.

In selling, we use physical skills: speech, tone, words, eye movements, facial expressions, body movements. We also can use touch (handshakes and pats, etc.). But because these are learned at such an early age, we forget the process we went through to acquire the skill of communication. In this way, there comes a time when we stop learning. By practising a skill, we move up the model to the level of high skill and high awareness. We do things in a deliberate way to bring about a physical performance. We know how to do it, but it has not become innate enough yet to stop thinking about it all the time we are doing it. To reach this level of competence takes a lot of practice. Think about your driving test. You are exhibiting a level of high skill, sufficient to pass your test, yet it can be and usually is tiring.

Carrying out a physical task and thinking about all of the movements associated with that task is hard work. It can be exhausting. Depress the clutch at the same time as easing off the accelerator. Check the mirror, while keeping an eye on your speed. Switch the indicator on, whilst looking at your wing mirror and the traffic ahead. Practice, practice and more practice will ensure you have high skills and low awareness, as it becomes second nature to you. Once you have passed your driving test, you quickly become a competent driver without thinking about all the stages necessary to start the car. And so it is with selling.

There are, of course, psychological issues to consider about practice and working hard (see **Figure 3**). Over a period of time, we settle at a level of performance that we feel comfortable with (A). This level could be high, low, or average, but the fact is we have great difficulty in moving significantly beyond that performance without some form of intervention by someone else, be that a manager, a trainer, or a colleague. For many salespeople, it usually involves moving to another company and starting off fresh (and most salespeople up to the age of 40 do so every three or four years). However, many could be as successful as their aspirations in their present company, if only they practised their sales skills more often.

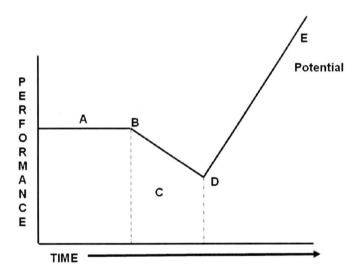

Figure 3: Performance over Time

The difficulty arises when that practice begins (B). If we have been performing at a particular level for some considerable time, then a training event is more than likely to have an adverse effect on our performance. Trying to improve someone's skills requires change and, as we know, change is not comfortable at any time, never mind change that involves learning to do something differently. It works well enough on training courses, but the vast majority of skills taught on formal training courses rarely alter behaviour on the job.

The reason for this is that learning to enhance your performance or learning to do things differently requires a significant amount of practice. During this period, it is quite common for performance levels to drop (D). If you play golf, you may understand the principle. Most amateur golfers play off a certain handicap score for years without seeing any dramatic movement in their handicap figure. Once in a while, they might be motivated to take a lesson from the golf club professional. Inevitably, the coaching given results in the golfer having to change a particular facet of their play. They might have to stand differently, hold their club differently, or alter the height of their swing. Whatever it is, both during practice and subsequent play, the golfer experiences a drop in performance. When this happens to a professional golfer, they continue with the practice until such time as the new or enhanced skill is mastered, eventually realising a higher overall performance level (E). The critical period for amateurs and many salespeople is during period C — which I call the Danger Zone. It's where things are not going well and they give up, returning to their previous performance level (A).

For all of us, learning involves a process of improvement, setbacks and plateaux. Professionals understand this; amateurs are fazed by it. Remember the adage: 'An amateur practises until he gets it right; a professional practises until he never gets it wrong'. Top golfers make it look easy, which belies the amount of practice they put into their game — both physical and mental. They may have played the game numerous times in their heads whilst walking the course before the game actually starts. Professionalism in golf, in common with all professions, is arrived at through a combination of knowledge, skills and attitude.

In selling, many salespeople seek to achieve professionalism only through knowledge, whilst others rely on innate sociability. They fall into two distinct categories: the competent technician who is a sales disaster and the sales genius who is a technical incompetent (**Figure 4**). The former group are those who are extremely knowledgeable but poor at communication, while the latter group are great communicators but lack knowledge. Clearly, there are others who appear to balance both, but they are and remain in a minority. The most common solution is to balance that difference through sales training. But that does not necessarily deliver new skills. Quite simply, salespeople need to practise skills, commonly known in other professional circles as 'skills drilling'.

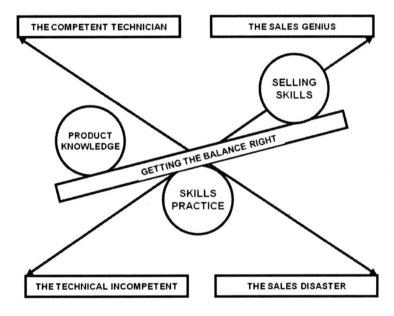

Figure 4: Getting the Balance Right

Perhaps the most dangerous combination is a successful salesperson with the associated traits of ego drive, empathy, and good social skills, but poor product knowledge. What this eventually produces are technical incompetents who can sell well enough, but are dangerous in that their lack of product knowledge and over-reliance on the need to succeed can have them selling products to your customers that may be totally unsuitable. Eventually, the customers vote with their feet.

ATTITUDE

Let us suppose that the sales job has been identified as requiring the skills of listening, questioning and presenting.

Is listening a skill or an attitude? Do people have poor listening skills because of a lack of training or a lack of interest? Is listening a matter of poor attitude or poor hearing? Are people bad at asking questions because they do not know how, or do they lack the motivation to find out about other people? Is presenting simply a matter of acquiring the skill to do so? What about people who are terrified to make presentations to groups of people (which has generally been found to be the case for most of us)? Is the manner in which people communicate a matter of training or of conditioning and, if the latter is true, can that be defined as being part of our personality make-up or attitude?

What is skill? Is it an innate ability that you are born with? Can anybody acquire any sort of skill? If most skills can be identified as being substantially influenced by attitude, can they be changed or enhanced?

It is certain that, barring physical disability, we all already can perform most of the skills that we are being asked to perform in a sales role. That is to say, we can physically perform those skills, given time, practice and feedback. So what stops us?

When I asked a number of sales managers this question about their salespeople, they came up with the following reasons:

- Wrong person for the job.
- Bad attitude.
- Not motivated.
- Useless.
- I did not pick them.

The last response is known as the 'inheritance factor'. You will also notice that 'attitude' appears again.

So if it's all about attitude, what can you do about it? Some people will say that you cannot change attitude, but I believe you can.

Festinger[6] has shown that, by changing behaviour, attitude changes are also possible. Obviously, it takes a long time, but then so does learning any new skill or changing firmly-held beliefs. By changing behaviour, a cognitive dissonance is created that is only relieved by changing attitudes to suit the new behaviour. People are not born with an attitude; they acquire one through beliefs and feelings and experiences throughout their lives and, in this way, attitude can be a dynamic entity.

As we get older, however, we take on board fewer attitude-changing beliefs, as we harden ourselves to the pain of change. Our background, our life experiences, and the past behaviours we see and adopt, together with the knowledge and beliefs we collect, determine our current behaviour and hence our current attitude (**Figure 5**).

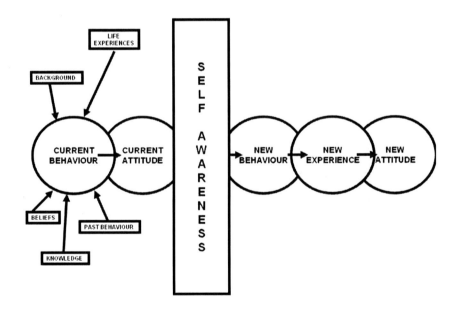

Figure 5: How Behaviour Shapes Attitude

Our attitude will be changed by an increasing self-awareness, which produces a new behaviour, leads to new experiences, and develops

---

6   L. Festinger, 'Behavioural Support for Opinion Change', *Public Opinion Quarterly*, Vol. 28, 1964.

into a new attitude. Mark Twain is reported to have said that, when he was 16, he was dismayed by his father, whom he reasoned to be probably the stupidest man in the world. Years later, he said, 'By the time I became 21, I was amazed how much my father had learned!'.

A good example of changed behaviour leading to changed attitude are those people who say, 'When we have children, we are determined that it will not change our lives'. Those of us who have children know how wrong is that premise. Whether we like it or try to resist it, the effect of having children, watching them grow, and feeling responsible for them makes an enormous difference to our lives. With hindsight, we would not say, 'It will not change our lives'. The fact is that the adoption of new behaviours gives us new values, feelings, and attitudes.

Acquiring self-awareness is not easy, but it is essential as a foundation stone for effective salespeople and indeed for coaches. Lasting change, and the self-awareness that sparks it, requires help. The most obvious choice is your coach. By helping the performer become more aware and by encouraging new behaviours, the coach can provide the spur to help you gain the sort of attitude that winners need.

Some successful salespeople might say that there is no need for further change or improvement: "I'm already a top performer, why should I need to improve?". However, if you continue doing things the way you have always done them in the past, is that enough? Is that enough when, for example, next year's sales targets are increased, or something changes in the business environment? Even the best can, and want to, improve their performance. A coach can help provide the impetus for improvement through an initial process of helping the salesperson become more self-aware.

Defining the right attitude is a complex issue. I often hear about having a positive mental attitude in sales and I would go along with the theory that positive people tend to be more successful at selling than negative people. It does, however, remain a theory. There are plenty of miserable salespeople who appear to be successful. However, attitude counts more than either knowledge or skills in isolation. A person with the right attitude will succeed in any case, but having both knowledge and skills rarely will work without the right attitude. Yet attitude has sometimes been confused with behaviour, and displaying a positive attitude perhaps could be just as effective as actually possessing one.

Perhaps salespeople need the sort of attitude that makes them want to learn more about their current attitudes and the way in which their behaviour affects others. Unfortunately, this desire to open the Pandora's Box rarely exists. Salespeople tend to be narcissistic and interested in examining their personality characteristics, but they soon become sceptical when adverse feedback is given, and seldom want to examine or have others observe their negative behaviour. To give an example: when a certain salesperson was given some honest feedback about his behaviour, this was his reply: "My behaviour has made me very successful in the past, and will continue to make me successful in the future. Are you suggesting that I will fail?". His coach said, "No. However, if I were to show that by modifying your behaviour, you will be 10 per cent more successful than you have been in the past, that would be helpful, wouldn't it?". He agreed. However, he failed to recognise a sale being made in the coach's question and his agreement. He subsequently failed to seize the opportunity to learn new skills, and ultimately failed in the job. It was not enough just to continue to do things the way he had always done them in the past.

WHAT'S IN IT FOR ME?

Let us suppose that a salesperson is identified as having a negative attitude. How can this be changed to a positive attitude? That's the big question to which all companies are seeking the answer. On the one hand, through perseverance, a coach or a manager can force behavioural change, which in theory will bring about attitudinal change, but most managers find it difficult to gauge whether an individual salesperson has accepted the need for attitudinal change or is merely feigning acceptance. From the salesperson's viewpoint, it is tempting simply to agree to improve either your behaviour or attitude when faced by a manager whom you know is not prepared to help you identify the root cause of your poor performance, but who simply wants instant action from you. And herein lies the crux of the problem. Change of attitude can take an inordinate amount of time. Unless the salesperson tunes in to the WIIFM (what's in it for me?) channel, it will not happen. It becomes even more difficult if it is something you attempt to do yourself without the skills of a professional coach.

A coach can help those who want to change and improve to do so, which brings me to the final point about attitudinal change. You have to want to. You have to want to change your behaviour, not just simply improve. Everyone would like to improve their performance, but wanting to change is a less desirable goal for most people. Your current behaviour delivers your current results. All top performers accept that it is their behaviour that delivers their current results. Therefore, in order to change your results for the better, you have to change your behaviour. This does not happen on training courses; it happens after the training course.

In a training environment, it is possible to motivate people to accept the need to change their behaviour in order to achieve improvement. But that motivation will last only as long as nothing happens to break the spell after the training event — such as breathing! It might last for a day or an hour. However, that hour may be just enough to make someone want to do something about changing instead of merely thinking about doing something. For it to work, however, you must have decided already that it is time you did something different. For many people and organisations, this is a paradigm shift in thinking.

A paradigm shift involves seeing things in a different way. The new paradigm sees a sales training course as help on the journey of change where, for example, you might initiate the process of greater self-awareness through 360° appraisal behaviour. You see your behaviour in the mirror but also benefit from feedback from your manager, and possibly your team and customers as well. But even this intervention is not enough for most. The new paradigm sees the coach helping you to draw up a realistic action plan, which you own and want to follow up on for improvement in your performance.

BARRIERS TO PERFORMANCE

In coaching salespeople towards improved performance, there are certain barriers that I have identified through research, workshops, and observation as common to salespeople in all types of industries and at all levels of experience:

- Low confidence and self-image.

- A low sense of personal responsibility for their performance.

- A low acceptance level of the need to practise selling skills.

Where many people make the mistake is in assuming that they can solve their overall salesforce performance needs by employing people with the opposite of these characteristics.

Only 15 to 20 per cent of salespeople are highly successful and the stark fact is that merely because people are successful elsewhere does not guarantee that they will be successful with you. The reason for this is that your management style may not be conducive to creating and retaining high performers.

Between 80 and 85 per cent of salespeople appear unable to overcome the barriers above. If you manage to attract salespeople who represent the other 15 to 20 per cent of top performers, you still have no guarantees that they will be as good or better in your team. You need to create an atmosphere in which they continue to feel self-confident, responsible and committed to continued learning about their products and how to sell them. Otherwise, either you may lose your high performers as they leave to seek a more challenging environment, or their performance may start to slide.

Most salespeople, whilst enjoying the perceived freedom and benefits of selling, exhibit internal conflicts that can affect their self-image dramatically, thus reducing their confidence. This, in turn, is transmitted to customers, bringing about a self-fulfilling prophecy of low performance. The beliefs that produce these internal conflicts include:

- **Hardly anyone chooses selling as a first career choice:** Most people drift into sales as other professional careers disappear through lack of opportunity or qualifications. If we consider that those in other professions tend to have made a more determined choice early on (some as early as primary school days), then is it any wonder that salespeople might be handicapped before they even begin? Indeed, choosing a career at an early stage has a distinct advantage. The majority of lawyers and doctors have received messages from their parents and educators about the need for application and commitment long before becoming qualified. But who is saying to students, "Apply yourself well and you might be able to make a career in selling"? Messages about self-worth and preferred career paths start early. We quickly learn that the term 'professional' is applied to a management cadre that excludes selling.

- **The route to professional status for salespeople is to become a sales manager:** Many believe that sales management does not require any high academic achievement and that promotion to management almost always is based on sales achievement. Many salespeople are able to produce short-term performance levels in order to retire into management. For many salespeople, promotion is a reward for successful selling, rather than an acknowledgement that they possess the knowledge and managerial skills required to create an environment that encourages high performance among their sales team. Therefore, many sales managers find it hard to manage their sales team effectively and are ill-prepared to realise the potential in them.

- **Salespeople and customers have the same feelings about selling in that the process is focused on benefits to the person selling, not the person being sold to:** Although many sales training theorists talk about creating an environment in which customers are encouraged to buy rather than having to be sold to, the way in which salespeople are trained, managed and rewarded rarely allows this to happen. We can recount all too easily stories of instances where service provided by an organisation falls far short of the customer mission statements contained in their advertising. This can lead to mis-selling with negative repercussions. In this way, whilst salespeople are trained to match their customers' needs to the company's products, messages about targets raise feelings of significant conflict once they are in the field and subject to the usual sales management pressure of achievement.

SO WHAT IS THE ANSWER?

The answer to professional sales success and how to coach salespeople does not lie in the sort of training needs analysis hitherto prevalent in most salesforces. I believe that the complicated sales training analyses and sales management practices currently being conducted in many companies are wasteful and ineffective. What is certain is that the plethora of solutions being offered to find, train, and develop the 'natural-born sales wonder' are being sold effectively, otherwise why would so many companies be buying those solutions, and why are there so many consultancies offering them? Yet here I am, peddling my own solution. The difference, I hope, is that this solution is based upon commonsense, 30 years of research, and is simple to apply, although I accept that it is not a quick fix, either in its learning or application.

SUCCESSFUL BEHAVIOURS

By the summer of 1999, having analysed thousands of sales calls over a period of 10 years, what emerged was a set of behaviours that I believe have a positive influence on the outcome of the sales process, and that the sales coach can use to help the performer to learn and improve upon. I have identified much of this behaviour to be attitudinally-based, and that the single most important influence on this attitude is the behaviour and intervention of the coach.

Story-telling (Social Skills) and Using Word Pictures

Having witnessed thousands of salespeople, I see a distinct difference between those performing at a high level and the rest. It took some time to analyse this difference, but eventually I realised that the conversational style used by high achievers differed significantly from their lower-performing peers. Whether it is in selling or in any other field, most of us have a predilection for wanting to listen to high achievers. It's not so much that they tell us about their achievements, but they phrase their conversation in such a way that makes us want to listen. You have heard of using word pictures, but how many people actually do it? Yet learning by pictures and story-telling is the essence of the way in which we acquire information today. Consider television or the Internet. Both are primarily picture-oriented, with a storyline underpinning each. Top salespeople display both sets of stimuli regularly. It looks innate, but it can be learned. Remember, top salespeople have learned the behaviour themselves. They may have a headstart because of background or experience, but nevertheless, as a coach you can help other salespeople acquire the same ability.

Probing Questions and Active Listening

An effective salesperson needs the ability to probe for information from the customer and to actively listen to the response. The former produces relevant information aligned to the customer's individual needs and the latter allows the salesperson to match products and services with those needs or, at the very least, know when to sell and when to stay quiet.

Whether the salesperson asks the right questions or bothers to listen to the answers is based upon attitude. Why else have questioning and listening been consistently identified as skills necessary for successful selling? Yet so many salespeople appear unable to do so. It is not because they cannot — it can be learned — it is because they do not have sufficient motivation to do so. They have not found enough right answers to the WIIFM question — what's in it for me? It is no good simply saying, "Well, that's your job", without additionally providing them with a motivational reward for having done that job.

I also caution you against the traditional training method of separating 'open' questions from 'closed' questions. I do not believe that simply asking "how", "what", "why", "when", "who" and "where" brings about open conversation, no more so than "Do you want this?" brings about a closed response. In exactly the same way that the vast majority of techniques for overcoming objections and closing do not work, simply learning words is not enough. You have to sound as though you mean it.

The phrase "I did not tell him to steal your purse" is simple and clear; yet each time you say it, a change of emphasis from one word to another can change the meaning completely. For example:

- _I_ did not tell him to steal your purse (meaning it was someone else).
- I did not _tell_ him to steal your purse (meaning I might have intimated it but I did not actually tell him).
- I did not tell him to _steal_ your purse (meaning I might have told him to borrow it or hide it, but not actually steal it).
- I did not tell him to steal _your_ purse (meaning I told him to steal someone else's).
- I did not tell him to steal your _purse_ (meaning I told him to steal something else).

Straightforward enough, you might say, yet how many people practise vocalising the difference? It is something that you as the coach can force people to do. Practice can help the salesperson make their presentation more effective.

One thing is certain: asking people the right sort of questions in the right sort of way draws people's attention and invites their trust and interest in you. By showing interest in others, they will reciprocate. This is the way for the salesperson with their customer, as it is for the coach with their performer.

Hard Work, Persistency and Never Giving Up

Ask any high achiever for the reason for their success and you will undoubtedly hear 'hard work' as a main response. The American baseball player Maurice 'Mo' Vaughan put it succinctly: "I have seen hard work beat good luck seven days a week". However, hard work on its own still is not enough.

Top salespeople rarely admit that they have a formula, but if you spend as much time observing top salespeople as I do, you will see a formula emerge.

I have already said that they tell stories, use pictures and ask questions that show interest in the customer.

They work hard, and yet research has shown that top salespeople see fewer customers than lower-performing salespeople, making a lie out of the myth 'see more people – be more successful'.

Besides preparing themselves more than their lower-performing peers, they give that bit extra by trying again and again. Top performers do not give up easily. They do not pester the customer; they just keep on building the relationship until eventually the customer buys. It would not be unusual to hear a top performer say, "I've been after this account for three years. I think I'm nearly there". Lower performers give up easily, becoming discouraged at the rejection.

Yet many salespeople bring about rejection themselves. What I have observed is that top salespeople do not back customers into a corner by asking them for a decision, no matter what. This does not mean that they ask open questions rather than closed questions. They simply appear more sensitive to the customer's indecisiveness by accepting personal responsibility for the customer's lack of commitment.

PERSONAL RESPONSIBILITY

Personal responsibility is the keystone to success and high achievement in all walks of life. There is no evidence, however, to support the theory that there are specific personalities more suited to sales than others. Salespeople are not born, they are made. Selling is not a matter of knowing the right techniques and tricks, and good salespeople cannot sell everything. The influence on each is the environment. As a coach, you are responsible for the environment you create for the salesperson. I observe that only 15 to 20 per cent of salespeople possess the attributes of a successful salesperson. The mistake is to believe that you can find and hire that small percentage. The problem is that many of the usual selection methods will not allow you to identify the 'natural-born sales wonder', because it is not possible to pick out specific 'winner' traits: success does not depend on gender, age, experience or personality. Despite the assurance by peddlers of personality inventories that it is possible to identify these specific personality traits, I would treat their assurances with caution.

Success is an outcome of behaviour. Most salespeople display low levels of confidence, personal responsibility, and the need to practise selling skills.

But there is no such thing as an all-rounder — it only exists as an average. None of us is average. Our attributes are balanced by our disabilities. To become better at selling, focus on people's attributes. In doing so, their disabilities will be crowded out. Coaching is the key to helping sales managers unlock the potential in all their salespeople. Sales managers who embrace coaching can make a big difference in the performance of their people. Part of your job as a coach is to weigh up the total package: the attributes and disabilities.

Make a call with regard to accepting people's failings compared to their attributes. While encouraging and nurturing the performer's attributes, you also will have to make a call with regard to their weaknesses. Are these failings development needs? Will the performer want to address them? Will these weaknesses adversely impact your sales team?

When I spoke recently to a successful football coach, he pointed out that sometimes you have to accommodate the player who does not conform: "If you let an eccentric star go because they are not following the rules, and you have not tried to harness their talents and manage them, you run the risk of them haunting you as they may go on to perform to a higher standard for the opposition". The difficulty always is in ensuring that the disruptive nature of non-conforming stars does not damage the equilibrium of the whole team, but then, all too often, sales managers are obsessed with creating a team atmosphere in an environment where everyone is judged on the same targets, not on their contribution to the team's efforts. On the other hand, if the star becomes too disruptive, then it might be better to let them go. In the end, someone else always will step up to the plate.

CHAPTER 3

TAKING A PROFESSIONAL APPROACH

*A competent professional listens well, probes, asks
questions, and thinks before he speaks. This is easy to
say, but hard to do. Jeffrey G. Allen*

WHAT IS PROFESSIONALISM?

When Allen made the statement above in 1998, he was talking about business in general. He could have been talking about selling. In the previous chapter, I said that good salespeople ask probing questions and they show they are listening. I also pointed out that good salespeople work hard. Allen was right: acquiring the habit of both is not easy, but then it has been said that nothing that is any good comes about easily.

Much has been said about professionalism in selling and yet we already know that almost no one chooses selling as a career. When I run workshops or seminars on the subject of selling, I often begin by asking people to write down what they wanted to be when they were at school. The room fills up with would-be doctors, solicitors, accountants, nurses, artists, footballers, and a thousand other occupations — everything except selling. In 25 years of research, I have identified less than one per cent of people who chose sales as a career. This fact alone is a major stumbling block in selling. People do not want to be in selling and therefore do not treat it as a profession.

I have been on numerous sales training courses where the trainers attempt to ingratiate themselves with the trainees by saying something like, "Your job is not different, is no less professional than, say, a doctor, or an accountant or a lawyer". Let's get one thing straight — for 99.9 per cent of people currently in selling, it could not be further removed from those professions. For one thing, there is no need to study; for another, there are no formal qualifications you must have before you can take up your profession. (This has changed in financial services as a result of legislative compliance requirements.) There is no apprenticeship and there are no recognised standards. Even though there have been significant moves over the last few years to improve the image and professionalism of salespeople — notably by the Institute of Professional Selling — selling as a profession on this side of Western Europe remains a doubtful career choice for your sons and daughters.

However, in most companies, salespeople are the single most important link with the customer. For many customers, the salesperson is the company. Yet within those same companies, being a salesperson is rarely seen as a worthwhile career. The commonly-held belief is that, if you have talent, it might be wasted in sales.

SELLING IS A PHYSICAL SKILL

Selling is not yet a profession in the true sense, though there are professionals who practise selling. In the same way, some would argue that sports is not a profession, but there are professional sportspeople. Apart from classical music, music itself may not be classed as a profession but there are professional musicians. Apart from ballet, dance in general may not be a profession in the accepted sense, yet there are professional dancers. Strangely, acting is seen as a profession. I say 'strangely' because actors become professional in very much the same way as sportspeople, dancers, and musicians, and yet appear to have more kudos than these counterparts. Why mention these professionals in the same terms as selling? It is because I believe that selling is the same. It is a physical skill and mastery of that skill through similar methodologies used by sportspeople, dancers, musicians, and actors will, and does, bring about professionalism.

I believe selling is a physical skill. There are some soft issues included, but the crux of a professional approach should be focused on those aspects that are in common with professionals such as sportspeople and athletes, musicians, actors and dancers. The dedication of these professionals is exemplified mainly through hard work and practice, things that are in short supply in selling. However, if I was to begin by berating salespeople for their lack of commitment and hard work, I would be met with a tirade of, "Oh no, not me. I work very hard. I put long hours in", etc. etc. Putting in long hours and working hard to what end?

CAREER CHOICE DICTATES A PROFESSIONAL APPROACH

There is also another important factor to consider about these professions. Earlier, I mentioned that less than one per cent of people choose selling as a career. If you ask the people in the professions of sport, music, dance or acting, what they wanted to be when they left school, 99 per cent say, "What I am now". In many cases, someone else fuelled their desire at a very early age. It could be a parent, grandparent, guardian, teacher or any number of role models. It will not be something they were born to do, it will be something they grew into, although the desire will have been developed and fashioned whilst they were more aware of their possibilities than their shortcomings. It is only later that we acquire doubts about our abilities. As children, we believe anything is possible.

The fact that these professionals have chosen a particular path in their lives gives them a significant edge over salespeople who have not. The former are more open to the rigours of the professional processes that I describe below. They are less suspicious of teachers (managers, trainers, and coaches) than salespeople are. They are better team players — they understand that more can be achieved by working together with other people. They focus on the positive, not the negative — they think about success, not about failure. There are more differences than similarities with salespeople, unfortunately.

And the raw material you are dealing with is often less than perfect. I often am asked by prospective coaches how to cope with salespeople who do not fit the perfect mould. The plain truth of it is that you simply have to work harder at coaching than your professional coaching counterparts have to, but then the satisfaction of achievement will be all the greater!

PROFESSIONAL PROCESSES

So what are these processes? The model below shows the elements that many professionals adopt in seeking to acquire and display top performance. I firmly believe that if salespeople understood, accepted and adopted these principles, they would deliver higher performance levels than they have hitherto. In addition, if you, as the coach, followed the basic principles that are laid out here, you would be taking the first significant step in releasing the power of your sales teams.

Figure 6: The Professional Processes Model

THE RULES

The model begins with rules. True professionalism comes from a starting point of accepting the rules within which the professional can perform.

In tennis, you might have heard John McEnroe complain about the ball being in or out, but not of the necessity to serve over the net. In football, players try to get away with infringements of the rules, but they know that they can expect to be cautioned, sent off, and even fined and banned for repeated fouls. All sportspeople know what the rules of the game are before beginning to play.

In music, Nigel Kennedy may have complained about always playing 'dead guys' stuff' but he does not change the notes of the music or leave parts out when he does play it. Musicians understand and accept that there are rules to music, one of which is that you play in tune. I can be the greatest guitarist in the world, but if I start playing in a different key to the rest of the band, I will soon be playing solo to empty seats. From jazz to traditional music, there are rules that must be followed by performers to avoid a cacophony.

Your job as a coach is to determine the rules that apply to your sales process and to have all the players (your salespeople) understand that their job is first and foremost to accept the rules, and then to apply them. For example, earlier I proposed that successful salespeople tell stories. If you believe that this is an integral part of your sales process that people should use, then either provide them with the stories or insist they develop storylines that you agree with before meeting a customer. If you believe that using word pictures or actual visuals will enhance your company's sales messages, then you should insist that pictures are used on every client call. You may also insist that they are of a certain quality. If you spend a fortune on developing visuals, then they should be used. All too often when I visit companies, I see cupboards full of brochures and presentations that someone has developed but nobody uses. When I ask the salespeople in that company why the visuals are not being used, they say that they are no good.

Picture this: I'm a player in a football team. The football league introduces a new ball. It's green and lighter than the one I'm used to playing with. I do not like it. What happens? I end up using it because that's my job. My job is not to design footballs. My job is to kick them to the best of my ability within the rules I have accepted. I'm a professional.

Your first job as coach is to identify and explain the rules of the sales game for you and your company. If the rules are too flexible, then you cannot coach. Think about the sales process as being contained within a total professional game. For example, if you were to view the arena in which the professional game of selling is to be played as similar to that of a tennis court, you might be able to visualise how the game would begin.

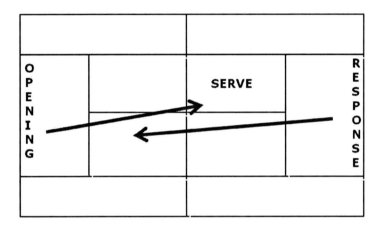

Figure 7: Selling as a Game of Tennis

For example, there is an opening (stimulus) and, from that stimulus, you hope to achieve a particular response. Therefore, you want to place that stimulus in a certain sector of the customer's court. Obviously, in this game there have to be two winners, but the principles of serving your opening and receiving a positive response do not infringe the rules of win-win. Your next step is to determine how you want the opening served. Is there something specific you want the player to say? Is there something specific you want the player to use to illustrate the story they have to tell? Is there a structure to the sales process that you want the salesperson to follow?

The salesperson's job is to follow the rules to the best of their ability, not to question them. Your job is to lay out the rules clearly so that everyone understands what is expected of them. The sooner you do this, the better. The best time is during the selection process, so that there is no misunderstanding when people start playing the game for you.

The sort of rules that might apply to your salespeople could include such things as:

- **Practising:** You might insist that your salespeople have to practise their basic openings at least once a day.

- **Implementation of policies, compliance and regulatory processes:** In some industries, e.g., financial services, the way in which the salesperson acts and conducts the sales process is highly regulated. You should insist that they observe the rules in this area at all times.

- **Being observed:** As a coach, you cannot determine how to help people improve if you do not observe them at work. They have to understand and accept that this will happen regularly.

- **Learning what 'good' looks like and copying it:** If you have determined what 'good' looks like, then your sales team must learn how to replicate it.

- **Consistency:** You can insist that they are able to deliver a basic performance to a basic level of competence whenever they are asked to do so.

- **Show the customer that we are listening:** The salesperson must be able to learn and deliver a performance based on active listening techniques.

- **A structured approach to the sales process:** You may decide that you want the sales process to follow a certain structure based on, for example, best practice. It is your right to demand that this is adhered to.

- **Understanding, accepting, and acting on the vision:** As part of your vision, you may decide that you want to operate in a particular market, or that you expect certain ethical standards. Your sales team, therefore, is required to follow these aims.

BASIC TRAINING

In order to release talent and ability, people must be able to learn and perform the basics, mostly through repetition and skill drilling. The important thing is for you to be able to say with certainty what it is that make up the basics.

When I have watched professional coaches in other disciplines, they seem to have no problems in deciding what is involved in basic training. When I watch business coaches, it is another story altogether. You must work out what is basic and what is advanced. Basic is what you expect people to be able to do and achieve as a minimum. You need to be able to decide how realistic it is.

For example, as a football coach, I want to see that you can kick the ball in the desired direction. I do not expect to have to show you how to do that. My scout will watch you play before I make a move to have you join my team. As a professional sportsperson, you will expect to be watched playing and to undertake a medical before joining a club. So why are so many salespeople offered jobs simply by attending interviews? Despite research showing that reliance upon interviewing as a means of determining job ability is about as scientific as throwing darts at a list of names, many companies still use interviewing as a predictor of job ability and of potential success in the job. I believe the reason for this is that many companies and sales managers have no confidence in their ability to identify what the basics of the job are. It is a prerequisite of sales performance coaching that you are able to identify the minimum standards required and to audition prospective candidates who wish to join your sales team to ensure that they can perform the basics. This is based on the premise that there are sufficient people in the employment pool who can display the basics — which is not guaranteed.

Too few sales managers have confidence in demanding to see a basic level of performance before coaching people to excel. You cannot coach people without seeing them perform the basics, which as we have previously explained, means that you too must understand what the basics are. Remember, it is your game and they are your rules, and if people want to play in your team then they have to play by the rules and be able to show you that they can perform the basics.

Basics for salespeople might include:

- **Sales selection interviews:** Ensure at a minimum that the job applicants go through a sales simulation exercise. For example, if they are required to sell home loans, you could ask them to sell you a loan in a structured role-play. In this way, you will be able to observe their sales strengths and weaknesses upfront.

- **Skills drills at sales meetings:** Instead of passing on information or doing tasks that could be done by email, fax or post, you should insist that the team practise their sales skills at each and every meeting.

- **Practice:** It is something that every professional except salespeople do. Your job as coach is to instil a practice regime, whether your salespeople want it or not. We already know they do not practise enough, which is why only 15 to 20 per cent of salespeople currently are exceeding target. There is no other profession where you are allowed to practise on a live audience other than as a salesperson or a sales manager.

- **Structure and scripts for customer approaches and sales situations:** Make sure that the individuals in the team can adhere to a structure at any time. A good time to check it out is just before a sales call — assuming you go on calls regularly with them.

- **Warm-up:** Every professional returns to basics just before a performance. In sales, we hear about the need to return to basics as though it was something unusual. Make it the norm by instructing your salespeople to warm up before every customer meeting.

Warming-up

The more you warm-up, the less chance there is of injury when you are performing. All professionals warm-up. Professionalism is not just about being paid to do something, although it is important to understand that, if you are paid to provide a certain performance, then you should do so in a professional manner.

Before salespeople give a presentation, they should warm-up, whether that presentation is at a conference, to a businessperson in their office, or to a customer at home. We usually associate warming-up with giving a presentation at a conference, although I have seen far too many presenters walk on stage without warming-up.

Warming-up should involve the physical process of selling. That means speaking the words aloud and, if possible, also making the actions that accompany selling, especially the opening. It is no good just thinking about what they want to say and do. To be truly effective and to give them the confidence they need, they should say the words aloud and accompany the words with the body language they intend to use.

That is not to say that mental rehearsal has no place — it is an important factor in its own context. Many top professionals use mental rehearsal immediately before the performance, when physical rehearsal is not appropriate; for example, it is pointless rehearsing a 100-metre run seconds before actually doing it. Some sportspeople (such as Jack Nicklaus) believe that mental rehearsal could be a 50 per cent contributing factor to success. It has been shown that mental rehearsal can stimulate physical processes and it helps us to see ourselves winning.

When professionals practise, they use the same skills and physical processes in practice that they do when delivering the actual performance. To deliver a performance of high quality, they have to believe that they are performing in front of others each time they practise.

I have observed that many salespeople have a great reluctance to use role-play. In most professions, practice plays a large part in developing skills and is the key to excellence in performance. In selling, however, salespeople steadfastly resist practising their skills. This resistance to using role-play also may account for the high failure rate among salespeople. It seems that salespeople get their practice in real sales situations. In order to be successful, salespeople require a high self-image. It appears that displaying inadequacies in front of their colleagues is either embarrassing or an indication of weakness. Salespeople are unlikely to rate highly any course that concentrates too much on role-play, and yet, as professional trainers, we know that it is role-play that determines how effectively trainees learn a new skill.

Remember that skills can be learned only through repetition and practice. It is only by practising something that we become aware of the potential length of the journey towards excellence. Practice and failure makes us aware of where we are. You may be disappointed if you fail but you will not get off the starting block if you do not try.

We learn skills through repeating them and our confidence and competence will grow. If you are learning selling skills, either you go on the same course again and again or you could do something about it yourself. One goal will not win you the golden boot. One composition will not make you into another Paul McCartney. One story in the local paper will not herald you as the next J.K. Rowling. The gap between simple ability and continuous performance is wide and deep and it relies on repetition. It is easier to turn in an average performance than to go for excellence. There is a direct correlation between practice and level of skill achievement. Remember our parents or mentors exhorting us in our youth that practice makes perfect, or, if at first you do not succeed, try, try and try again? Unfortunately, commonsense is not always common practice in sales.

Does that mean that you have to aim for perfection for yourself and your salespeople? Certainly not, unless you define perfection as trying to be the best you can be. Perfection, by my definition, is not attainable. That is not to say that some people fool themselves into believing that they have achieved it; whether they admit it is another matter. There are those people who ease into a comfortable performance — they stay in their comfort zone and, in performance terms, stand still. Standing still and delivering the same performance may be acceptable in their organisation. In fact, the 'standing still syndrome' is quite usual in top performers. For many people, performing at a level above colleagues is what it's all about: "So long as I can keep a step ahead, that's all I want".

As I said earlier, however, the people performing at a high level also have great feelings of insecurity. Being out in front is just as stressful as being way behind. In many ways, being out in front can be more stressful. In their minds, there is only one way to go — down. At least the person at the bottom, having hit bottom, can say that the only way now is up. In a lot of ways, coaches have more difficulty getting top performers to increase their skills, ability and performance than they have with low performers, and yet the same process and rules apply.

USE OF TOOLS

Most professionals have tools that they use and they also understand that the way in which those tools are used requires compliance with basic rules. An actor knows that they have to use a stage prop in a certain way at a certain time, and they know that they have to stick to the script. A dancer uses a certain type of footwear specific to a particular dance style. They accept that they have to perform a number of steps in a certain sequence. A guitarist knows that they have to strike the strings of a guitar in a particular fashion and hold the strings on the fret board in a certain way in order to comply with the music — which they follow.

The tools of selling might include such items as:

- **Sales reports:** These allow the salesperson to determine their current level of performance in relation to where the sales manager wants them to perform.

- **Training packages:** Salespeople can use these to practice the basics.

- **Sales presenters, visuals, brochures, and point-of-sale systems:** They have to be used in a certain way. For example, you do not simply give a brochure to a customer to read, you take them through it, highlighting the important points you want to make. If using a particular point-of-sale system (e.g., a presentation constructed on a laptop computer), you might want to ensure that the customer sits in a certain place whilst you present.

- **Development journals:** Does each salesperson in your team have a personal development plan? If not, then it is time they did. Where else do you record what training has been given, how the trainee has reacted to that training and what they have learned?

THE ROLE OF THE COACH

Once performers have experienced the benefits of practice and structure, and eventually the release of talent and personality, it becomes a natural development to reach for constant improvement. Yet it is not that easy — there is a missing element.

Whenever I ask senior managers the reason for one team performing well and one not so well, the answer is inevitably "The difference is the manager". My own experience and research over the last 20 years bears this out.

The major influence on sales success is provided by the behaviour of sales managers, not salespeople. It took me quite some time to come to this conclusion, so perhaps I need to emphasise it again – the difference between a high-performing sales team and a low-performing sales team has nothing to do with the salespeople in the team – it has to do with the sales manager.

In common with other professional groups, changing the manager changes group performance for better or worse. It is the same with sport. A chairman of a premiership football team put it succinctly: "I have always said that, in any football club, if you have only a limited spend, spend it on the best manager you can. Everything is down to the quality of the manager".[7]

Yet, in most cases of poor sales performance, the first casualty is usually the salesperson. Even though you may have set the scene with regard to rules, basic training, the use of tools, and the need for consistency and inflexibility, you additionally need to understand that, without the desire to improve, people always will deliver below their potential. The key to unlocking potential is the coach.

Professionals understand and welcome the involvement of the coach because they recognise that they will not achieve their potential without the intervention of a coach. Whenever top performers are asked to comment on their success, inevitably they refer to the coach. For example, in the Heineken European Rugby Championship in 2000, the Munster rugby team were rank outsiders but stunned everyone by reaching the final. Team members all alluded to the influence of the coach, Declan Kidney, when reflecting on their team's success.

I have observed hundreds of people performing their jobs, where it is possible to see how those with the desire to improve their physical delivery, in time, have improved the outcome of their job. Likewise, I have seen those with emotional barriers say things such as

---

[7] *The Irish Times,* 26 August 2000.

"I've always done it this way. I cannot do that. I cannot say that". As a consequence, these people continue to deliver a poor performance and deliver less-than-acceptable results.

Your major message to your team has to be about the need for constant improvement. How you construct and transmit that message is covered in the next chapter.

CHAPTER 4

FROM SALES MANAGER TO SALES COACH

Treat other people the way you would wish to be treated,
and never forget what it was like to be managed.
Frank Salisbury

BEHAVIOUR BEGETS BEHAVIOUR

The way in which the salesperson feels about the job they do has a major impact on their effectiveness, but that is not the whole story. Mostly, sales managers are drawn from the population of salespeople and therefore bring with them the same baggage they acquired in their sales role. Although many want to treat their old peer group in a different way, few have been shown any other example other than the *status quo* of 'there are those that lead and those that follow'. Indeed, most sales managers take up their new positions without any instruction, formal or informal. They then adopt the behaviours their past managers have taught them, perpetuating the *status quo*. It seems that, whilst everyone else in the world must be trained to do a certain job, managers undergo some form of metamorphosis over the weekend they move from being a salesperson to becoming a sales manager.

Insofar as personal responsibility is concerned, I found that most sales managers believe that they are responsible for the success of their teams. Whilst they are certainly accountable, no one can be responsible for the performance of another person. It is a difficult and complicated lesson to learn but it represents the foundation stone of professional performance coaching. I have already stated that the major influence in the attitude of personal responsibility needed for success is the coach. How you behave towards the salesperson ultimately dictates how they feel about themselves, but you are not responsible for their individual performance – unless you have created an environment in which they are bound to fail.

Messages about self-worth, preferred career paths, and the nature of authority start early. We quickly learn that we generally have to do as we are told, that people in authority have the upper hand, and that the term 'professional' is applied to white-collar work, excluding sales. In addition, the lessons about being personally responsible for decisions and success begin too late to have any effect.

By the time most people begin their first job, the way in which they relate to authority has become embedded. Unlearning these patterns of behaviour requires a significant effort on the part of both the employee and, especially, the manager. Remember, managers themselves have been subject to the same history. By the time they arrive in a management role, they have convinced themselves that their position of authority now bestows upon them the responsibility to change others, whereas as Argyris[8] rightly said as far back 1962: "No one can develop anyone apart from himself. The door to development is unlocked from the inside". It is as true today as it was then.

MANAGEMENT INFLUENCE

Each person is responsible for their own personal performance. Each person can become better at a particular skill today than they were yesterday. For many people, however, improvement goals are usually set for tomorrow: "I'll start that diet tomorrow ... as soon as I get the exercise bike ... after I come back from holiday ... when I've finished this packet of cigarettes". Personal effectiveness and responsibility for performance improvement only really happen when dealt with within the immediate time-scale. In order to acquire, improve, or retain a skill, there has to be desire, commitment and determination to actually do something now.

What I have found is that managers find it difficult to understand why it is that so many of their salespeople appear not to have that

---

[8] Chris Argyris, *Interpersonal Competence and Organisational Effectiveness*, Tavistock Publications, 1962.

same sense of responsibility that they themselves display. Yet I only observed it as a natural phenomenon in less than 20 per cent of the sales population anyway. Paradoxically, it is this 20 per cent that is 'farmed' to produce the current sales management population. It would be akin to promoting all of your best football players in a team to be managers. There is a significant body of evidence in these professions to suggest that taking the best professional performer is no guarantee that they will make a good performing coach. As Professor of Marketing at the University of North Texas J.K. Sager said in 1991, "The best coaches were seldom the best players".

As you move from selling into sales management, no doubt you will be exposed to a great number of theories and purported effective practices of management. Each will be accompanied by a recipe for managerial success, rather than realising that the answer to sales management success lies within the behaviours of their current salespeople, not in quick fixes. Despite this fact, there are as many sales managers failing each day as there are salespeople. As with sales success, there remains a constant search by trainers, managers, and the jobholders themselves for the secret of sales management success and apparently the money to pay for it. Enormous sums are spent yearly on management training and development, but recent surveys show that less than a third of top and middle managers feel that they learned anything important, whether the training was conducted within their own company or through outside courses and consultants. The figure for positive ratings for in-house training looks particularly bleak, at less than 10 per cent.

For many salespeople, a successful period in a front-line sales role is merely a pre-cursor to a sales manager's position and often is the only mechanism available to keep them in the company. There is no guarantee that successful salespeople will be good sales managers but one thing I believe is certain is that managers have to be able to sell. In fact, I believe that there are three basic skills that sales managers must possess to be successful as a sales coach:

- They must be able to sell.
- They must be able to train.
- They must be able to motivate.

ABILITY TO SELL

If you want to be successful in sales management, you must know how to sell. You must be able to get yourself in front of people and then make a sales presentation that will make people buy from you. The other factors like training and motivation revolve around the basic principle that the sales manager knows how to sell. You do not have to be number one, or even in the top quartile, but you will struggle to sell your role as sales coach without having had some reasonable success in a sales role. Then you can empathise with the salesperson. Empathy is important in selling and it is important in sales management.

Now this may appear to fly in the face of what I have said elsewhere, which is that, to be a good coach, you do not necessarily have to be able to do the job you are coaching people in. In fact, sometimes, it is more effective not to know too much about the job you are coaching, as this makes you ask what might appear to be stupid questions, but in reality are often the questions that get right to the heart of the issue. A recent confirmation of this appeared in *The Sunday Times*,[9] regarding the well-known English rugby coach Dave Alred. In his article, the reporter talks about how Luke Donald, the golfer, was being coached by Dave Alred, the rugby coach. Although unusual, it tends to be accepted that being able to coach in one sports discipline enables you to be able to coach in another, as the skills are the same. When Alred began working with Donald, the golfer was ranked 29th in the world. By the time the article was published, Donald was ranked 3rd.

The problem in selling, because the acceptance of coaching is not endemic, is that resistance is widespread. That is not to say that coaching is not widespread, because it is. However, I contend that its acceptance at an emotional level is not widespread, and that means there is a lot of faking of acceptance going on. There may come a time when this changes, however I am not convinced that it will be anytime soon. In the meantime, in order to overcome this resistance, sales coaches must demonstrate experience of selling in order to

---

[9]   David Walsh, 'The Guru', *The Sunday Times*, 6 March 2011.

penetrate the emotional resistance by salespeople to be coached. Yet my own experience, because I tend to insist on a holistic approach to sales coaching, is that it does work, and work well. This approach is covered in detail in **Chapter 6**.

ABILITY TO TRAIN

Sales managers must be able to train. Even so, the thing that works best in sales training and what makes the difference is the trainer. It is the person who does the training who determines the success or failure of a sales training programme. They must have first-hand experience of the subject. If you have not been in selling, you are not going to be a good sales trainer. If you have not been in sales management, you are going to struggle in relating to trainee sales managers. Without first-hand experience, you will only know the topic at a theoretical level. The line manager, acting as sales coach, from time to time must run training sessions in the field. They are also the only people who have the authority to force changes in behaviour, which is ultimately what you are attempting to do.

If managers generally are promoted because of past performance levels, then it seems folly not to use their knowledge and skills to train others to the same levels of high performance. Whilst this may seem obvious, many companies see training and coaching salespeople as a staff trainer's role and move managers into administrative functions for which most are ill-suited.

Surveys[10] into sales and management training clearly show a disappointing reality about the lack of effectiveness of sales training. The fact remains that most skills training does not last or make any impact on the bottom line. The need for training is widely recognised but the difficulties of making it measurably effective are great. The implication is that sales management are not providing the right climate for creativity to flourish and, given the regularity with which new techniques in marketing and promotional methods appear, it will be increasingly necessary for sales managers to initiate programmes to stimulate their sales teams to adopt a more creative

---

[10] 'The Sales Direction Survey of Sales Management', *Sales Direction Magazine / Management Exchange Ltd*, 1989.

approach to the development of sales from their territories and accounts.

However, the simple reality is that, unless some management action is taken to prevent it from happening, new skills acquired in formal classroom situations deplete to vanishing point in a few short days unless the manager creates tasks to provide the opportunity for the newly-trained salesperson to use new skills.

ABILITY TO MOTIVATE

What motivates salespeople is debatable. Is it possible to give people self-motivation? I believe that it is, although there are few people who can do it. It may sound strange to say that salespeople have to be motivated to want to succeed, but my experience shows that salespeople devote more energy to fear of failure than to the desire to succeed.

Success in selling is a mixture of external and internal factors. The external factors come with the job and include knowledge, experience and — more than anything else — the influence of the sales manager. Internal factors are those things that come from inside — self-motivation and the right attitude. You cannot guarantee that all new starters will arrive with evidence of either on the surface, and it is the sales manager's job to get trainees to dig deep within themselves and find the motivation that should be there.

In 1987, Kovach[11] produced a paper that examined the results of previous research into employee motivation. The factors swung from 'the need for recognition' as the main motivator to 'having interesting work to do'. I favour the work carried out by Shipley and Keily[12] in the early 1980s, which shows that salespeople are motivated by reward, recognition and achievement.

Winer and Schiff's research in 1980[13] found that salespeople placed a high priority on financial reward as a main motivating factor in job

---

[11] K. Kovach, 'What Motivates Employees?', *Business Horizons*, September 1987.

[12] D. Shipley and J. Keily, 'Motivation and Dissatisfaction of Industrial Salespeople', *European Journal of Marketing*, Vol. 22, No. 1, 1988.

[13] L. Winer and J.S. Schiff, 'Industrial Salespeople's Views on Motivation', *Industrial Marketing Management*, 1980.

performance. Making more money was specified as an important motivator. If reward is the primary motivating factor for salespeople, then you must link your training with that by getting trainees to establish, early in the training event, what it is they want from the sales job. Your training should be seen as a method of obtaining just that reward.

The point of all this is that sales trainers and sales managers have a joint responsibility to motivate people to want to learn, but to do that, everyone needs to fully understand the problems presented by closed minds and negative attitudes. Somewhere along the line, in your role as a trainer and a sales manager, you must create your own stories and analogies. They do not come out of books or exist in other people's training notes. They come from experience, and especially from the experience of having been there yourself. Good sales trainers and sales managers have a history of both success and failure, and are prepared to share those experiences, especially with new employees.

Most sales managers still find the subject of how to motivate salespeople a complete mystery. Levinson's article[14] on the subject is particularly revealing. He says that motivational theory is hardly sparse and most executives will have studied the subject in depth at some time or another:

> Many have taken part in managerial grid training, group dynamics laboratories, and seminars on the psychology of management, and a wide range of other forms of training. Some have run the full gamut of training experiences; others have embraced a variety of panaceas offered by quacks.

But like much skills training, he believes that the expectations of companies that their people will change after a training event, no matter how senior they are, is totally unrealistic, and I could not agree more:

---

[14] H. Levinson, 'Asinine Attitudes towards Motivation', *Harvard Business Review*, Jan/Feb, 1973.

Furthermore, it is one thing to become aware of one's feelings; it is quite another to do something different about managing them, let alone managing those forces that affect the feelings of other people. Experience is not enough; training in a conceptual framework and supervised skill practice is also required. Sales managers need to be wary of adopting blanket motivational approaches, and concentrate more upon the individual.

MANAGERIAL BEHAVIOUR

The important thing to consider is that people learn from how managers behave, not from what they say. When I facilitate training for managers, I usually conduct the following self-awareness exercise. I ask participants to think about a manager for whom they used to work who they would describe as a poor manager, then to consider what it was that manager did, said, and how they behaved that made them a poor manager, and lastly how it made them feel. The responses I have received include that the manager was:

- Never there.
- Unapproachable.
- Patronising.
- Apathetic.
- Selfish.
- Uncommunicative.
- Unpredictable.
- Inconsistent.
- Always telling lies.
- Only interested in results.
- A bully.
- A sexist.

I then ask them to describe a good manager for whom they have worked. The responses include that the manager:

- Listened.

- Had time for me.
- Showed empathy.
- Asked my opinion.
- Encouraged me.
- Gave both freedom and responsibility.
- Kept commitments.
- Gave firm guidelines and expectations.
- Was approachable.
- Created a good team atmosphere.
- Rewarded with praise and with money.
- Believed in me — I had no limits.

Unfortunately, there appear to be more poor managers than good managers and we tend to learn more from poor managers than from good ones, the reason being that poor management is easier to execute. It takes less time. Being a good manager is difficult: it requires hard work. My contention is that good sales coaching equates with good sales management.

MOVING FROM SALES MANAGEMENT TO SALES COACHING

Much of sales management is an instructive process. This is extremely important for groups such as new starters. Although there are many theories of motivation, one important theory — Douglas McGregor's Theory X and Theory Y[15] — forms the foundation stone of sales performance coaching.

The manager as coach must have complete belief in the potential of individuals, with the proviso that the potential of those individuals is limited to the performer's desire, commitment, and physical possibility. It is said that we only use a fraction of the skills we are born with, in the same way that we use a mere fragment of the potential of our brains.

---

[15]   D. McGregor, *The Human Side of Enterprise*, McGraw-Hill, 1960.

Those of us who have experience of sales management might recognise that, at some stage, the high aspirations we had for some salespeople did not materialise. Perhaps they let us down, perhaps we let ourselves down, or perhaps it was just bad luck. Perhaps the theory did not turn into practice and all the role-play in the world did not prepare you for the real world. The latest fad was just that — a fad. There are bound to have been times when you returned from a management training course full of ideas and ideals, keen to try them out on the troops. Some of those ideas never got off the ground, and others, well, at least you can say, "I tried that once and it did not work".

In the meantime, life goes on, people come and go. You have successes and failures and either you make it to the top, settle somewhere round the middle, or have already sunk into obscurity. And the effect you have on other people? Who knows? How many come back and tell you? Yet there is a way for you to get what you want by helping others get what they want, and the mechanism allows both parties to feel good about the process. The process is sales coaching, but what does it mean?

COACHING IS NOT TRAINING

For most people, the term 'coaching' merely has replaced the word 'training' as a means of teaching or instructing people. Already, many trainers and managers talk about their coaching programmes when what they really mean is their training courses. Training is a vital ingredient for any sales coaching process, but training is not coaching. We train people to do the job, we coach people to excel. Sales training and sales coaching are not divorced, however. Almost every time a sales coaching session has been conducted, a sales training session will inevitably follow, and *vice versa*.

The purpose of sales training is to teach the salesperson a skill, which normally is acquired at a very basic level on a training event. The mistake many people make is to assume that a training course will teach people anything other than the basics. The acquisition of new skills only ever can be achieved through significant repetition, and there is rarely sufficient time on a training course to accomplish it. This is why the coach's job following a training course is to ensure that sufficient time is allocated for the trainee to practise. Skills are embedded through practice and repetition (**Figure 8**). The skill can then be improved by means of sales coaching.

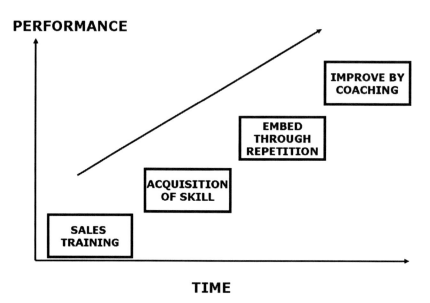

Figure 8: The Sales Training Process

Training is a two-phase process – foundation, and workplace induction. Foundation training is simply a process by which the organisation provides the new salesperson with a basic set of skills and knowledge required to fulfil the job role. Also understand that whether the salesperson is experienced or not, they need to attend foundation training. The experience they bring with them, whilst relevant and pertinent in previous organisations, most likely will need to be adjusted to fit in with the new organisation.

CONTROL

Inherent in the philosophy of coaching is personal ownership and responsibility. Recent research has found that managers who suffered from stress, when pressed, realised that the stress was a result of their feeling that they lacked control. They accepted their own management responsibility, but found it difficult to accept the blame for poor performance of subordinates when they had tried extremely hard to help poor performers to improve.

An example from the athletic world is that, having coached an individual to a record-breaking time in practice, and subsequently the same record-breaking time was delivered on the track, how responsible should the coach be if another athlete delivers a faster time? Obviously, what other people do cannot be dictated — perhaps planned for, but not dictated, and certainly not coached for. Also, what personal responsibility could the coach have if the athlete tripped during the race? Obviously, none.

Let's look at an example. In the Melbourne Olympics, Alan Storey, coach to the Irish athlete Sonia O'Sullivan, summed it up well when referring to her preparation for the big race:

> All I can do is put Sonia on the starting line as fit as it's possible for her to be and then hope she runs the race as quickly and as cleverly as she can. She'll finish first or second or third, but if she does not, it will not be because she wasn't properly prepared. It will be because there are better people in the race.

Sonia came second in the 5,000 metres. It was not as good as first but it was better than thousands of other hopefuls. The coach did all he could. Sonia took personal responsibility for her own performance.

What about in a work environment? If a person has been coached to deliver a performance in a negotiation situation, and someone else delivers a better performance, what personal responsibility should the coach shoulder? The same answer applies: none.

However, in business, as in sport, the coach ultimately may be accountable. In sport, the coach may not be able to take their team to the Olympics. In business, the coach may be beaten at the negotiation table and, subsequently, the firm may suffer. That accountability goes with the job.

The problem is that many managers confuse responsibility with accountability. Responsibility is a personal thing and can only be attached to those things over which you have direct control.

Sometimes, for the best of reasons, most times because it is easier and quicker, managers take on board the personal responsibility of completing a task, either by telling people specifically what to do, or by doing part of or the whole task themselves. It is normal when the manager is absent for the task to be completed to a greater level of efficiency by the team, who enjoy the freedom to express themselves without interference.

THE TRADITIONAL ROLE

There is a difference between managing and coaching. Most people do not like to be managed, although it is an accepted facet of being at work. Coaching is generally not well known at work and, therefore, for most people the jury is still out on accepting coaching as a workplace practice. What has emerged, however, as I have implemented sales coaching programmes, is that many people appear to associate coaching with some kind of remedial activity. I have heard expressed that, if someone is receiving coaching, then they must either be slow or under review.

Coaching in other professional fields such as sports could not be further from the suspicions expressed by many people in business. Whereas many people find being managed a disabling experience, coaching is an enabling experience. Coaching releases talent and ability.

Traditionally, managers are seen as focusing on end results. The traditional model for management (**Figure 9**) is one in which managers seek to push people from their current performance to the company's desired performance levels. The focus for both manager and salesperson is usually the desired performance. In many organisations, desired performance is considerably higher than current performance. Inherent in this continual focus on target is failure. Many recent surveys show that people at work are unclear as to the company's objectives and where they fit in. Target-setting is usually an arbitrary process, having already been decided some time before any manager–subordinate discussion takes place. Managers have a tendency, which is reinforced by management training, to regard forecasting and objective-setting as their remit, and whether operating in a democratic fashion or not, only occasionally will involve subordinates in the process, by which time it is often too late to make any difference.

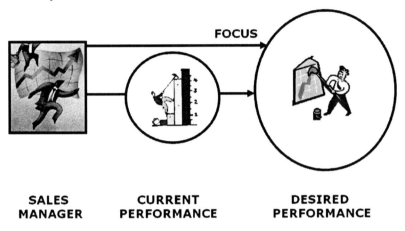

SALES   **CURRENT**   **DESIRED**
MANAGER   **PERFORMANCE**   **PERFORMANCE**

Figure 9: The Traditional Management Model

THE SALES MANAGER AS SALES COACH

There is another way to improve performance. Acting as a sales coach potentially can produce significantly higher performance levels than any other form of management. Sales coaching can reduce levels of stress in management, and produce the sort of working environment for everybody that, as yet, has not been experienced.

The main function of a coach is to develop a person's potential. The way in which that is achieved is to focus on moving forward step by step. This is known as the principle of whole – part – whole (**Figure 10**). Our performances are made up of parts. The skill lies in being able to describe those parts in detail so that they can be broken down into skill sets that can be worked on. By focusing on one part of the total performance and working on it to make it bigger, when that part is put back into the whole, the performance will increase. It is a simple enough principle, yet easily missed by both performers and managers.

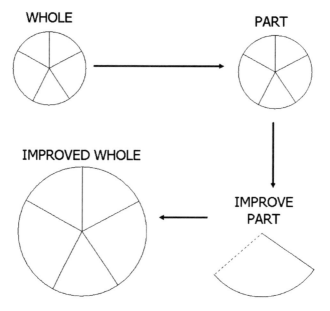

Figure 10: The Principle of Whole – Part – Whole

In this way, the new style of sales manager as coach (**Figure 11**) is about taking the first step towards performance improvement – pulling the salesperson towards to the goal rather than pushing. The focus of performance improvement is to take the first step.

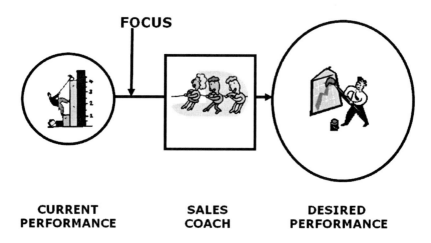

Figure 11: The New Style of Sales Manager

BENEFITS OF COACHING RATHER THAN MANAGING

There are a significant number of benefits to be gained from sales managers adopting sales coaching as a preferred style. These include:

- The job of the sales manager becomes easier, as salespeople take responsibility for improving their skills levels.

- It enables a higher level of delegation, thus allowing the sales manager more time to manage rather than doing the work themselves.

- It increases productivity, especially when salespeople know what the goals are and how to achieve them.

- It helps to build the reputation of the sales manager as a developer of people.

- It means a sharing of responsibility for performance.

- Positive recognition and feedback increases salesperson motivation.

- Regular sales coaching sessions negate the need for one-off yearly appraisals.

- A sales coaching environment encourages risk-taking and creativity.

- Teams run by sales coaches feel more of a team spirit.

- It can reduce labour turnover – salespeople feel good when they are exceeding at work. Even when offered more money, many salespeople choose to remain with their current organisation if they believe that they are learning and being developed.

- Relationships are enhanced – whenever top performers have been surveyed regarding their opinion of their line managers, their comments have been less than charitable. In particular, many salespeople feel that sales managers have little or nothing to contribute to their success. By adopting the role of sales coach, the line manager is seen as a contributor to success rather than a detractor.

CHAPTER 5

WHAT DOES IT TAKE TO BE A GOOD COACH?

*Always bear in mind that your own resolution to succeed
is more important than any other one thing.*
Abraham Lincoln

FROM SELLING TO COACHING

There are some widely-held beliefs about sales coaching that I would like to expose, namely:

- **Manipulation and sales coaching are the same thing:** This is not true. Professional sales coaches are able to get people to work for them in ways not necessarily for their own good. However, they also help salespeople recognise areas of mutual interest that can produce benefits for both parties.

- **Giving it your best shot is all that really counts:** This is not true. Too many people substitute effort for accomplishment. The reason for the sales function and the sales coaching function is to get results. You can help salespeople to work smarter, not harder, but the bottom line is what really matters. Working hard is not enough.

- **Empowerment is the same as delegation:** This is not true. Delegation is telling someone what you want when you want it and how it is to be done. Empowerment is about helping salespeople to understand, through your behaviour, that they are responsible for their own action and that it is those actions that bring about results, good or bad.

- **Sales coaches have to come from the ranks of top salespeople:** This is not true. A sales coach is not a person who can do the work better than others, but is someone who can get others to do the work better than they can.

- **Sales coaches must control all situations:** This is not true. Tight control mechanisms restrict personal responsibility in salespeople.

LOOKING IN THE MIRROR

At the end of this chapter, you will find one of those questionnaires that people seem so interested in completing. I include it with tongue in cheek. On one level, it may help you to determine how good you are; on another, it may encourage you to try harder. The chances are, however, it will have little effect. I maintain that self-awareness, or looking at your behaviour in the mirror, is a critical element of performance improvement, whether you are a salesperson or a sales coach. The problem is that, given the choice to become aware of our shortcomings, we all tend to choose self-analysis rather than critical feedback from someone else — and self-analysis is far from accurate. As John Hillier, the CEO of the National Council for Vocational Qualifications, said at a conference I attended a few years ago: "I can convince myself I am in control of my weight, providing I do not go anywhere near the scales".

What happens is that we tend to protect ourselves from criticism by not putting ourselves in the position to be criticised. Most of us would say "I do not mind criticism, providing it is objective and not personal". The fact is that all criticism feels personal, yet it has to be said that the only valid feedback is that which is given by someone else, someone who is qualified to do so. So far as salespeople are concerned, that means you, the coach. This means that, insofar as your salespeople are concerned, you have to sell the idea that they need feedback, and that the best feedback will be from observation. It is not enough to rely on the performance of the practice pitch to judge real performance. What happens on the practice pitch is only ever a rehearsal at best. The measure of any true performance happens on the pitch. At any rate, the questionnaire and the feedback on profile has been used by many managers we have met, who would all say that it has helped them to focus on changing their attitudes towards their perceived coaching ability. But then, they would say that, wouldn't they?

VISION

Lincoln's statement, quoted at the start of this chapter, is true no matter what your calling is. We have already seen, however, that the existence of a resolution to succeed is not on the surface of everyone's 'performance potential iceberg' (**Figure 1**). It is probably there but, for many people, it has to be unearthed. Who better than the coach to do this? Common to all successful teams, whether in sports or in sales, is a leader with vision, purpose, and a desire to achieve.

This book is not about goal-setting, but setting goals does have a place in coaching. Whether the individuals in your team already have defined their goals or not, you need to consider what your own goals are and how you intend to influence the team in achieving them. You must find a way of expressing your goals so that the individuals in your team adopt them, and your goals must become their goals.

If self-awareness is the first thing that a successful coach needs, then the second is a vision. Every leader should have a vision of where it is they want to be. Every coach has to have a vision of what it is they are trying to achieve. You also need to be able to express it in a way that influences others to invest emotional and physical time in achievement of your goal. You need to bring your vision to life and it should be something that you can constantly refer to. Most of us will have a tale to tell about some teacher in our past who was responsible for either firing up our interest in a particular topic, or damping it down. Parents sometimes are astounded by children who appear to acquire an aptitude for a subject not previously on the family agenda.

Before constructing your vision and the manner in which you want to communicate it, you need to be aware of the direction in which the company is going. Does your vision reflect the vision of the company? Having conducted this exercise on a number of occasions, I have found that, in 99 per cent of cases, the sales message that the executive starts out with rarely reaches the customer other than through advertising (**Figure 12**). The more layers of management there are, the more the message begins to be distorted, with the only consistent message from the top to the bottom of the organisation being achievement of target. This is clearly not customer-focused.

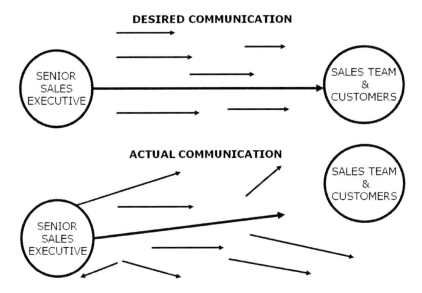

Figure 12: How the Sales Message Reaches the Sales Team and Customer

By the time the message reaches the sales team, the training department has constructed it into a process which, whilst promoting a particular way of selling in the classroom (if at all), is never followed up in the field. This, in turn, allows the salesperson to adopt whatever sales process they wish — which they do. Because communication is confused from the top to the bottom, most salespeople simply make it up as they go along. The top five to 10 per cent have a formula for success that they use and know works but which they cannot describe. When asked to do so, they rely upon the same mythology as their lesser-performing peers.

Your vision statement should not be just about the journey; it also should contain messages about how you intend to get there. You need to find a way to explain how you intend to implement the professional processes referred to in **Chapter 3**. In addition, you must find a way in which to bring your message to the attention of your sales team by employing the same methodologies you want them to employ with the customer – for example, story-telling, word pictures, or personal experiences.

Your vision should inspire people and contain some examples of where you have overcome the odds in the past to succeed. It is no good expecting people to follow you if they think that you have never achieved anything before or they get the impression that you are making it up as you go along.

You need to give your salespeople the impression that you will succeed, whether they are with you or not. Your commitment to success must be explicit. Whether people buy into your vision initially does not matter. What is important is that you believe in it and are seen to believe in it. You will find, as you consistently strive to achieve your vision, that people will join in.

It is also important to vocalise your vision. It is no good just writing it down and sending it around the troops. Too many company vision statements are plastered on the walls of organisations which have little or no meaning for the great mass of people working in those organisations. Tom Peters states that:

> Visions come from within as well as from outside ... Posters and wallet-sized cards declaring the vision and corporate values may be helpful, but they may not be. In fact, they can hinder and make a mockery of the process if the vision and values are merely proclaimed, but not lived convincingly.[16]

In one survey,[17] 85 per cent of workers questioned expressed no confidence in the quality of the company's leadership or the vision they had been fed. Yet in the same survey, 90 per cent of those workers said they were committed to giving their best. The environment in many companies, however, works against the release of potential.

---

[16]   Tom Peters, *Thriving on Chaos*, Macmillan, 1987.
[17]   MORI Survey, *People Management*, 1 October 1998.

CREATING A POSITIVE ENVIRONMENT

We are all products of our environment. I have already expressed the view that salespeople are not born, they are made. It is the environment that we work in that produces people who succeed or fail. You are the major influence in that environment. There may well be many things that are wrong in your company, yet it is a fact that the main influence on any worker is that person's line manager. This is nowhere so true than of salespeople and sales managers.

The environment can, and does, change everyone. It either reinforces what we believe and causes us to respond, or it takes us by surprise and produces an adverse reaction. I found a startling number of salespeople who had experienced the 'when I started on Monday, it wasn't the same company' phenomenon. I also found a correspondingly large number of sales managers who experienced the 'when they started on Monday morning, they weren't the same person I had interviewed' phenomenon.

The problem is that far too few recruitment and selection criteria are made on an examination of skills and behaviour, and far too many decisions are made on personality and interview alone. The environment that you create for your salespeople starts with the selection process. Besides testing the skills and behaviours you want to see in a salesperson, the selection process is where you lay out your expectations. You should make it clear what is expected of the new salesperson before they start, and what they can expect of you. For many professional coaches that I know, the expectation of success is a primary tool in the arsenal of success they have. I call it the self-fulfilling prophecy.

THE SELF-FULFILLING PROPHECY — THE PYGMALION EFFECT

Managers communicate their expectations of people in a number of ways, both verbal and non-verbal. Even managers who believe in the potential of their team and who say something positive about the work of their subordinates need to pay attention to the tone of their voice, the manner in which they look at others, the general lack of concern shown in their body posture; otherwise, they can impart a totally different meaning to their team.

Managers can, and often do, communicate both negative and positive expectations to others by saying nothing. Giving employees the 'silent treatment' or the 'cold shoulder' tells people more about what the manager is really feeling than a load of meaningless words. It is not what the manager says that counts, it is the way they behave.

What managers expect of employees and the way in which they treat them determines their performance. Low expectations bring about low results; high expectations bring about high results. Experiments conducted in the 1960s by people like James Sweeney, Professor of Industrial Management and Psychology at Tulane University, and J. Sterling Livingston, Harvard Professor of Business, confirm the existence of the 'Pygmalion Manager'.

Some managers treat their employees in a manner that results in superior performance, whilst others treat their subordinates in a way that elicits poor performance. The unique characteristic of superior managers is that they have, and transmit, high performance expectations of their charges, which are fulfilled. In study after study, encompassing such companies as Metropolitan Life Insurance Company, AT&T, West Coast Bank and the Texas State Employment and Education Agency, the existence of the Pygmalion effect was found. Managers were told that certain groups of employees had been tested and found to be of superior quality than others. In each case, the groups thus identified performed at significantly higher levels than the control groups. In reality, the groups had been picked at random. The only factor that led to increased performance was the way in which the manager treated the individuals in the identified groups.

In one particularly remarkable experiment, Robert Rosenthal and Lenore Jacobson told a number of teachers in a secondary school that, following intelligence tests, 20 per cent of the children had been found to be intellectually superior to the others. Follow-up tests confirmed that the 20 per cent in fact performed higher than the rest of the school. The disturbing fact was that all 20 per cent were chosen at random, and that, when asked to rate the high achievers, the teachers said they were more attractive, appealing, and better adjusted than the rest.

Rosenthal identified four factors that he says influence the Pygmalion effect:

- **Climate:** Managers who create an encouraging social environment that includes warmth, attention, smiling, and appreciative non-verbal signals.
- **Feedback:** Managers who give more specific verbal messages about employees' performance, who give more sincere praise, and even criticism when appropriate — all of which assist the employees in improving their performance.
- **Input:** Managers who stretch employees by giving them more difficult tasks and help them to learn more.
- **Output:** Managers who encourage questions, allow staff time to develop, and give people the benefit of the doubt.

The people most affected by the Pygmalion effect are young workers and those new to the job. New people, in particular, are dramatically influenced by the way in which the manager treats them and introduces them to the workplace within the first few weeks of employment.

The characteristics displayed by Pygmalion managers and coaches are:

- They have belief in themselves and confidence in what they are doing.
- They have belief in their personal ability to select, train and motivate people. Even when they pick the wrong people, they rarely give up in the attempt to improve them.
- They have an ability to communicate their positive expectations, which are both realistic and achievable, to their employees. Setting unrealistically high goals for employees only leaves workers dissatisfied and accepting far lower results than they would have achieved on their own.

- They have a belief that people can make their own decisions in life and at work. They encourage workers and empower them with the authority and responsibility for achievement.

- They prefer rewards that are a result of the achievement of their subordinates, not of their own achievements.

In my own surveys, when I have asked salespeople whether the job had matched up to their expectations, 65 per cent of people said it had not. The challenge is clear. Managers must learn to believe in themselves before they can inspire others to believe in them and, as Rosenthal says:

> We still do not exactly know how the Pygmalion effect works. But we know that often it does work, and that it has powers that can hinder as well as help the development of others.

More recent studies continue to highlight the all-important role played by the line manager in the relationship with their direct reports and their commitment to the company. In the 1990s, the Gallup Organization undertook large-scale research on employees' commitment to their companies. The research showed a strong relationship between employee commitment and productive outcomes, including productivity, profitability, and customer satisfaction and employee retention. It is not surprising to learn that an employee who is committed to the company is more productive and provides higher-quality customer care. The question is: "How can you help your sales team to be more committed?".

The Gallup research revealed that the relationship between employees and their first-line managers or supervisors was key to creating strong commitment towards the company and the job and, in turn, to generating the four productive outcomes highlighted above. Good managers are prepared to put a lot of effort into creating positive relations with those they supervise. They set clear and reasonable goals, provide feedback, give praise and help their employees' growth and development.

A sales manager who acts as coach can create this positive learning environment. More important than any financial incentive, recognition and encouragement of individuals and teams will engender loyalty and commitment. Big targets will not create big results. Sales coaching breaks up a task into small steps and looks at how each individual's performance can be encouraged and improved, so that longer-term targets can be reached and even surpassed.

QUESTIONING SKILLS

Coaching is essentially a questioning skill. In later chapters, I will outline key questions to help you use the POWER© coaching model. However, simply becoming better at questioning belies the atmosphere and environment needed to obtain right answers from the questions you ask. The difficulty is that, as a manager, you have the authority to ask questions of the salesperson. Similarly, the salesperson has a duty to answer the questions, but whether they do so willingly, openly and honestly is another matter.

Some people would have you believe that you have to ask open questions that encourage people to talk, as opposed to closed questions that cause people to answer yes or no. This sounds good in theory, yet in practice it may not happen.

Neuro-Linguistic Programming (NLP) exponents may be right to claim that the barriers to successful communication are our perceptions, emotions and past experiences. There are two fundamental elements to communication, namely stimulus (the information which is sent and therefore begins the communication event) and response (the way in which the information is received and the reply). On the surface, this appears straightforward. NLP practitioners believe that a potential barrier to effective communication could be the fact that you might not be offering the customer the information in their preferred format. They say that you should take time to test in which media format the customer prefers to receive information.

Those three media are:

- Audio.
- Visual.
- Kinaesthetic.

The theory behind the third expression purports that kinaesthetic people prefer to deal with feelings, and that by focusing your questions on the other person's feelings (e.g., "How do you feel about that?"), the communication will be more open.

It is said that, through observation, listening to responses and general analysis, we can arrive at the ideal medium that best suits the other person. This might work if you have a lot of time and a degree in psychology. For the rest of us, it is sufficient to realise that messages we send can be forgotten quite quickly by the receiver. In addition, it might not even arrive in the same format you wanted it to, simply because of the potential barriers that exist to communication. You may think your message has been conveyed accurately, but because of different perceptions, the recipient's understanding might be totally different, and therefore they respond unexpectedly. Words mean different things to different people. Remember how the example 'I did not tell him to steal your purse' can mean different things, depending on how the words are spoken.

The recipient could have recently experienced an emotional upset. If they have something else on their mind whilst you are trying to coach them, you may believe that you have the solution to all of their performance problems, but you might not be getting an effective hearing.

Effective Questioning

To be 'effective questions', they have to do two things: raise awareness and generate responsibility in the performer.

Sir John Whitmore[18] describes how, during a golf coaching session, he asked a trainee to tell him whatever she noticed or felt when she first swung at the ball. He wanted her to focus her mind and to find out where her attention was focused. He then reflected her words back to her. This checks your understanding and lets the trainee explain further if necessary. He confirmed with her that she wanted to produce 'a more fluid swing', and followed her interest. He did not introduce his own agenda — she retained responsibility. He asked her to focus on her swing. He then helped her to narrow

---

[18]   *Coaching to Improve Performance*, Training Video, Performance Consultants, London, 1998.

her focus and raised her awareness even further by first asking her to describe, on a scale of 1 to 10, how fluid her swing was, and then at what point she noticed any awkwardness. The whole process was then repeated as the trainee focused on different aspects of her performance.

The coach asks questions in order to raise awareness within the performer, resulting in improved performance and then a sense of personal responsibility for future action. In this context, raising awareness means gathering appropriate information to a high quality. Often, the information we need to solve a problem and improve performance is already available to us. We are simply too distracted by other things to focus on it.

John Whitmore says that, during the coaching session with a trainee, he helped her to focus her attention and to raise her awareness so that she was able to "gather appropriate information to a high quality" about her own performance. She did the rest — to a large extent, subconsciously.

Because raising awareness is such a critical part of this process, the coach avoided doing anything that would divert attention. He never interrupted. This would have destroyed the focus and reduced awareness. He also discouraged the trainee from 'trying harder'. Trying too hard is actually counter-productive, because it focuses attention on trying to do something instead of being aware of what is happening.

David Whitaker says that, when coaching in a business environment, he follows precisely the same principles. Raising awareness of reality became not just "What's happening as you swing the golf club?" but "What are you experiencing in this business situation?".

David Hemery[19] (who trained me in the GROW model of coaching) was asked whether there was a risk that, in letting people work out their own solutions, you might be seen as abdicating responsibility as a manager. He said that, in this context,

---

[19] Olympic Gold Medal Winner of 400 metres hurdles at the Mexico Olympics in 1968. Not only was Hemery the only British Gold Medallist at these games – but he also set a world record.

responsibility means the decision by the individual to undertake a task and see it through to completion. To generate this responsibility in the other person as a coach, you have to resist several very strong temptations. You must not:

- Lead the other person.
- Force your own agenda on them.
- Push your own solutions.

One of the major benefits of coaching in this way is that the coach or manager generates the responsibility for improved performance where it belongs — with the person who will do the job. This is delegation, not abdication, and it leaves the manager free to do their own job better.

LISTENING SKILLS

How can we hope to be good coaches if we do not know how to listen? In a coaching context, we need to develop empathic listening skills; that is, skills that enable us to understand not only what the person is saying to us, but also the emotions and difficulties that may underlie what is being said. If we fail to gain an understanding of someone's attitude and beliefs, then we cannot begin to identify the barriers to performance and thus we cannot help that person to begin the road to improvement.

It is estimated that, in an average working day, people spend 9 per cent of the time writing, 16 per cent of the time reading, 30 per cent of the time speaking, and an astonishing 45 per cent of the time listening to other people. If we think about how much time we were allocated at school and in further education to learning how to write, read, and speak, and compare that to how much time was devoted to learning how to listen, perhaps we can begin to understand why we are so bad at listening to each other.

Ask yourself: "What were you taught about listening?". The answer typically is "Nothing". Yet all salespeople know that they are supposed to listen to their customers and to identify their needs. Furthermore, sales managers and salespeople in general have a firm belief that they have little time available for all the things they have to do. This perception of the pressure they are under also contributes to poor listening skills. One of the more common complaints that employees have of their managers is that 'they do not listen'. For some managers, effective communications will have a better chance of happening when they fight off the need for their ego to dominate. Instead of feeling that, as the boss, they have to do all of the talking, they should give listening a chance to succeed.

Teaching listening skills should be a prime requisite of any training event concerned with the personal development of communication skills. We have two ears and one mouth and we should use them in the correct proportion!

How good a listener are you? Poor listening skills are very damaging to both the sales and coaching process. As a coach, poor listening will cause frustration, distrust, defensiveness and clamming up on the part of the person being coached. You will have lost an opportunity to truly diagnose a performance problem or realise an opportunity with the performer.

Barriers to effective listening include:

- Tiredness.
- Preoccupation with another problem.
- Disagreeing with the speaker.
- Disliking the speaker, for whatever reason.
- External noise or distractions.
- Feeling physically uncomfortable.
- Thinking ahead.

Empathic listening means that we should listen to what someone is saying with an open mind. We need to suspend judgement, stop comparing the speaker's experience to our own or drawing comparisons with other members of the team. Quite often, people who are in a coaching situation feel nervous and find it difficult to put their feelings into words. The coach must be able to listen beyond the words being used to hear what is unsaid in a person's heart and mind.

One of the biggest obstacles a coach may encounter in interpersonal communications is the tendency to compare or interpret people's messages on the basis of the coach's own experience and attitudes. A coach may advise, question, interpret and evaluate a person's story on the basis of the coach's own standards of performance or those of other members of the team. This is unhelpful and ignores the individuality of the person being coached.

The next time someone is talking to you, observe your own reactions. Are you giving that person your full attention? When someone is telling you a story, are you thinking, "Yes, that reminds me of when ..."? You will be amazed at how difficult it really is to listen with an open mind and to give someone your full concentration.

Effective listening needs 'will and skill'. You need to want to listen and be really interested in what someone says. Remember, you cannot fake it because your body language will give it away, particularly your eyes, and so you need to practise the skill of listening.

In an interpersonal communication, who is working harder: the one who talks or the one who listens? Stephen Covey[20] confirms, "The one who listens does the most work, not the one who talks". I would also concur with him that to be heard and understood is the psychological equivalent of breathing air.

In order to build up a trusting and open relationship in a coaching situation, not only should you listen, but you should also show you are listening. Develop your listening skills by:

- Concentrating on what is being said.

- Ignoring distractions.

- Thinking about what is being said, not how you will respond.

- Asking questions to make sure you understand fully.

- Summarising to show that you have the full picture.

- Checking back with the other person that you have captured the essence of their message before giving your views.

---

[20]   Stephen R. Covey, *The Seven Habits of Highly Effective People,* Simon & Schuster, 1991.

Show you are listening by:

- Maintaining eye contact with the speaker.
- Taking notes.
- Not interrupting, arguing or blaming.
- Using reflective statements that indicate awareness and understanding of the other person's feelings without indicating whether you agree or disagree with them.
- Using brief assertions such as very short statements (e.g., "I get it"), sounds (e.g., "hmmm") or gestures (e.g., nod your head) to let the other person know that you are listening.

The Effect of Not Being Listened to

In order to highlight what it feels like not to be listened to or understood, you can try the following short exercise with your sales team. Prior to an event, do not tell people what the content of the session is to be. Arrange the group into a circle. Pick a subject, any subject, for discussion. Allow the first person in the circle to make some comment, in a clockwise order, of no more than one minute about the topic. Then ask the second person to summarise what the first person said. The first person must agree that the second person has accurately captured what they actually said. If the second person has not captured the first person's point, then the first person must repeat the point and the second person must again try to summarise it to the satisfaction of the first person. Once the point has been correctly captured, the second person is free to make their own point. In turn, ask the next person to summarise what their colleague has said. Follow the same rule as in the previous exchange. Continue around the circle. Most will have forgotten what the previous person said, or simply not paid attention in the first place, as they will have focused more on what they were going to say.

After the exercise, ask each person what it felt like not to be understood. Then ask them to reflect on some sales situations where the customer was not listened to, where their needs were not really identified or understood. What can they learn from this? The same lesson applies in a coaching situation, where it is essential for the sales manager as a coach to try to fully understand the performer by asking questions and by effective listening.

In a follow-up listening exercise, divide your group into pairs; instruct each person to ask their colleague questions about themselves and then try to listen effectively to their answers. Then alternate the roles between speakers and listeners. The ensuing discussion should bring out how much better you feel when people ask you questions about yourself, and how good it feels to be listened to by someone who appears interested.

When we look at the POWER© model of coaching in greater detail, you will get another chance to see how probing and listening skills can support the coach in developing a high-impact coaching session. These skills do need significant practice, however, before your interpersonal communications become an 'unconscious competence'.

Telling is Not Coaching

It is less effective to tell someone what to do or how to do it than it is to ask them in a coaching situation what needs to be done or how they feel having done something. In sport, striking a golf ball involves a combination of movements involving your whole body. There are several aspects to it, from addressing the ball, getting your body comfortable, settling your grip through to using your mind to focus on the shot. The performer learns best when the golf coach asks them questions with regard to how they feel holding the club and their body posture, rather than telling them in the first instance that they look awkward. This is comparable to a review of a sales interview.

When the sales coach has observed the salesperson in an interview, it is far more effective to review their performance afterwards by asking them at different stages what went well, how it felt at a particular point and how comfortable they were using their sales aids. Telling instead of asking appropriate questions can result in a lack of understanding of the sales process by the performer and provides less of an insight into what they did that worked and what exactly they need to improve upon.

When the sales coach asks questions of the performer, rather than simply starting the review by telling them how they got on, it leads to the salesperson digging deep within themselves for internal answers. This in turn leads to a higher self-awareness of their own performance and a truer understanding of the ingredients of success.

NON-VERBAL SKILLS

Communication experts estimate that only 7 per cent of our communications are represented by the words we use, while 55 per cent of our communication happens through our non-verbal body language, with the remaining 38 per cent coming from the way we speak and the sounds we make. Effective coaches need to be aware of how they ask questions, emphasising key words. For example, when agreeing an action plan with the performer, the coach might place greater vocal emphasis on the word 'when' in a phrase such as "When will you start work on your areas requiring improvement?". Similarly, the coach needs to pay close attention to the performer and how they answer the coach's questions. For example, if the performer does not sound convincing with regard to actioning their improvement plan following a coaching session, then the coach should probe further with a reflective statement such as, "You do not sound fully committed to the action plan".

However, it is the non-verbal communication, our body language, which is most important. In our body language, we convey our feelings most honestly, so if we are saying something we do not believe, our body language often will contradict our words.

Good coaches get as much response from people by not saying anything than by saying too much. For example, sometimes the use of a pause in a dialogue by the coach should encourage the performer to provide more information, or an encouraging nod of their head often will have the same positive result. Coaches need a strong knowledge and understanding of body language. Aspiring coaches should read as much as they can about the subject, and receive as much training in body language as time and resources can afford.

While body language is beyond the scope of this book, there are two areas in particular that are of great importance to coaches: facial expression and touch.

Facial Expression

We learn by seeing. The majority of all information we take in is through visual stimuli. The old saying goes 'a picture paints a thousand words'. We cannot see words, only pictures, which is why it is important to learn how to paint pictures in people's minds. Learning to communicate visually is vital. We do it anyway, whether we are aware of it or not. The problem is that where is a discrepancy between what we say and what we communicate by our face or body posture, people will always believe the body language, not the words. It is therefore very important for the coach to be tuned in to reading the performer's facial expressions. Do these facial expressions confirm what the salesperson is saying in response to your probing questions or do they suggest that the salesperson is not fully sure? Facial expressions can prove quite insightful.

Touching

Touching is something most people never receive any training in, and yet it is an important function of the coach's communication toolkit. It has been shown that tactile people are more likely to be liked than non-tactile people. Having said that, touch is also a matter of culture. In Ireland and the UK, touching sometimes can be seen as a taboo: "This person is invading my personal space!". Yet in places like France, Italy, and Germany, touching between consenting adults is very acceptable, especially in greetings. In Germany, if you fail to shake hands when you meet someone, it could be construed as being standoffish and, in some circles, extremely rude.

If you body-watch, it is fascinating how most people avoid being touched, and yet those who engage in tactile behaviour look far less repressed and more open. It is the last bit — openness — that I want to focus on here.

It is important when building a coaching relationship to establish open behaviour. Openness in terms of what can be said to each other and — just as important for the person being coached — what can be attempted. A coach often will encourage someone to try things they have not tried before, and which therefore potentially may make them look and act foolish. Unless a completely open relationship has been established, then the person being coached will feel reticent about trying something new. Touching is merely one additional part of a total communication system that coaches can employ to help them establish a supportive relationship with the people they are coaching. Touching is therapeutic and supportive. It is comforting and encouraging, and, used correctly, can enhance positive communication. Used properly, it will be unnoticed by the person being touched.

It is vitally important that, at the start of each meeting, the coach shakes hands. It breaks into the personal space, and immediately establishes a close working relationship. Likewise, shake hands when parting, and if possible reinforce the handshake with a light touch on the elbow. Touching the elbow when giving a verbal message adds credibility to the message. When touch is accompanied by a supporting verbal message about the worth of the individual, or an encouraging message about carrying out some practice whilst the coach is away, it will add value to the message.

The two other places to touch are the upper arm at the back, and preferably the back of the shoulder which is simply backslapping, congratulating people for a task well done, or an attempt at something new. Two light taps are sufficient.

Having said all of this, it is important to note that most research into body language focuses on West Europeans and North Americans. You need to acknowledge and understand the culture and context of the environment in which you are working and, through this, to analyse whether the body language the salesperson is using is appropriate and effective for the situation.

OBSERVATION SKILLS

As in sports coaching, the coach must become a keen observer of the individual's performance in order to be able to provide valuable feedback on how well they have done, or to highlight shortfalls in, for example, their sales interview technique.

Nothing drives home the problems associated with individual perception and the difficulties of acquiring consistent observation more than a recruitment interview panel. It is rare to find two people watching the same person being interviewed who will have the same views, or even see the same performance. Yet good observation skills are a vital component of good coaching. The coach must be objective in feedback of performance, and as such must be able to help the person specifically recall any item that requires attention. For a manager new to coaching, this is one of the toughest things to do. The best way to instil this skill is through repetition and practice.

The best way to demonstrate the truth of this is by getting together with a few of your coaching colleagues, undertaking observations of the same events, and comparing notes. By recording a simulated sales interview on video and playing it back, you all could present individually your opinions on what the salesperson in the interview did well and poorly. Do this first without examples and without discussion. Write each of your opinions of the salesperson up on a separate piece of flipchart paper and put the charts on the wall. It is guaranteed that there will be discrepancies, many of them major. Then each of you should justify your opinions by quoting examples of behaviour. Your other colleagues then should be allowed to contribute their own findings. Each observation that becomes a point of dispute should be reviewed and resolved by playing the video interview at the appropriate point.

If you have a bank of video interviews, so that this process can be repeated a number of times, so much the better. The main points to derive from this should be the need for:

- Clear criteria against which to judge the salesperson.
- Simple but precise note-taking on what exactly was said.
- The importance of analysing how the sales messages were delivered. For example, the use of body language and tone of voice is very important in order to get a full understanding of what has been said.
- No judgements without examples.

Good coaches are caring, supportive, have good listening skills, are as much aware of their own strengths and weaknesses as those of their team, have good verbal and non-verbal skills, and are good observers. These are skills that can and should be practised, as they form the basic elements of a coach's communications toolkit.

PATIENCE

Coaches need to develop patience. Learning can be a slow and sometimes uncomfortable process and, when you have explained something to a salesperson a number of times, it is essential that you do not lose your temper if they still have not understood the point or the feedback given. Smile and develop the patience of Job. Explain the point again and help them to understand. Behaviour will not change unless there is buy-in from the performer. Changing behavioural habits can take about 28 days before the new sales behaviour becomes ingrained.

When your sales team fails or falls behind in achieving their goals, advise them that you believe in them, remind them of the endgame, what is in it for them, and encourage them to renew their efforts. Where mistakes are made, try to see them with your team as valuable learning points. In this way, you are role-modelling and your team will learn from you the need for patience with their own efforts. Rome was not built in a day. Patience in coaching is a virtue, but it is also an essential attribute for the coach.

HOW WELL DO YOU MATCH UP AS A COACH?

Have a look at yourself in the coaching mirror by answering the following questionnaire. A number of coaching situations follow. After each situation is outlined, a choice of three alternative reactions is suggested. You must rank the alternatives in order, where '1' is your first choice, '2' is your second choice, and '3' is your third choice.

Situation 1: The salesperson you are coaching has under-performed for some considerable time. You have been unable to spend any time with them due to pressure of work elsewhere, but at last you have arranged to allocate a day's coaching with them. This is the start of the session.

Item	Alternatives	Ranking
1.1	There is a problem here with your performance. I'm here today to help you resolve that, and together I'm sure we will succeed.	
1.2.	We seem to have a problem here with your performance. What do you think the answer is?	
1.3	I see my job today as helping you to perform better, no matter where the starting point is. What do you expect of me today?	

Situation 2: You have arranged for one of your salespeople to come to see you. The purpose for you is to arrange a coaching session with them. Their performance has not been good in the recent past.

Item	Alternatives	Ranking
2.1	I want you to arrange to show me how you do your job so that I can help you improve your performance. When would be the best time?	
2.2	My intention is to accompany you on the job regularly so that we can improve your overall performance. I'd like to come out with you tomorrow.	
2.3	So, why do you think I've asked to see you?	

Situation 3: You have identified a situation in which a member of your team is performing badly. The individual concerned comes up with an idea to improve performance.

Item	Alternatives	Ranking
3.1	That seems like a good idea. Do you think there is any down-side to it?	
3.2	Well, it looks alright on the surface, but I think you may have a problem implementing it.	
3.3	That's good. Is there anything else you could do?	

Situation 4: Following a coaching session, you have agreed a course of action with the salesperson. You now want to implement it.

Item	Alternatives	Ranking
4.1	When do you propose to put this plan into action?	
4.2	What I suggest is that you try this out and come back to me within 7 days and tell me how you got on.	
4.3	I now need to watch you implement this plan, in order to provide some feedback. When are you going to do it?	

Situation 5: The salesperson steadfastly has been unable to identify any personal improvement plan. According to them, they are trying as hard as they can.

Item	Alternatives	Ranking
5.1	What exactly is it that you want to do?	
5.2	What have you done so far, and what effect has that had?	
5.3	It looks as though you might not be suitable for this job.	

Situation 6: During the initial coaching discussion, you know that the salesperson is looking at the wrong problem.

Item	Alternatives	Ranking
6.1	It seems to me that you are looking at the wrong area.	
6.2	Do you want my opinion as to what the real problem might be?	
6.3	On a scale of 1-10, what is the likelihood of that course of action working?	

Situation 7: The salesperson has tried to implement the agreed plan, but there has been no improvement in performance.

Item	Alternatives	Ranking
7.1	What exactly did we agree, what did you do, and what happened?	
7.2	OK, so that did not work. What else could we do?	
7.3	Perhaps you did not try hard enough.	

Situation 8: Just before meeting the salesperson, you were given information from someone else who highlighted the performance problem as deriving from a personal situation at home.

Item	Alternatives	Ranking
8.1	I seem to sense that perhaps there is something wrong at home.	
8.2	Is there something troubling you that you have not told me about?	
8.3	What's happening for you at the moment?	

Situation 9: This is now the sixth time you have met and, on each occasion, the salesperson has failed to implement agreed action plans.

Item	Alternatives	Ranking
9.1	For this relationship to work, you have to keep your part of the bargain.	
9.2	Why have not you done what you said you would?	
9.3	I've tried my best to help, but it's a hopeless case.	

Situation 10: The salesperson seems incapable of implementing what has been discussed. The only alternative to you seems to be to show them how to do it.

Item	Alternatives	Ranking
10.1	Look, I'll show you how to do it.	
10.2	Do you want me to show you how to do it?	
10.3	Where do you feel the main difficulty is in implementing this action?	

Situation 11: When you asked the salesperson whether they had any more ideas, they said they could not think of any.

Item	Alternatives	Ranking
11.1	I might have some ideas, but it's up to you if you want to hear them, the only proviso being that whilst they work for me, they might not work for you.	
11.2	So what do we do now?	
11.3	Come on. Try again.	

Situation 12: When you asked the salesperson to say what they wanted to do, they said "Anything you want – you are the boss".

Item	Alternatives	Ranking
12.1	I want you to start doing your job, that's what I want.	
12.2	What do you want?	
12.3	What do you think I want?	

Situation 13: Your boss asks you why it is taking so long to improve one of your team's performance. You have the feeling it will never improve.

Item	Alternatives	Ranking
13.1	I have the feeling it's never going to get better.	
13.2	It's up to him. We just have to be patient.	
13.3	He's now had long enough. I'm thinking about asking him to leave. What's your opinion?	

Situation 14: The salesperson has tried very hard to implement the plan, but they do not seem to be moving forward. They say "It's impossible, I might as well throw the towel in".

Item	Alternatives	Ranking
14.1	What effect will that have on you?	
14.2	That's quitting. I thought you were made of stronger stuff.	
14.3	Well, that's up to you.	

Situation 15: During a particularly bad coaching session, the salesperson tells you that the reason they cannot perform to standard is that there is a difficult situation at home, which is affecting their concentration.

Item	Alternatives	Ranking
15.1	What do you want to do now?	
15.2	We've all got problems. The important thing is not to let it affect your work.	
15.3	I think the best thing is for you to go home and sort it out.	

Situation 16: The salesperson is having difficulty implementing the performance improvement suggestions you have made. They say

"Look, every time I have a problem, you ask me a question. You are the manager. Just tell me what to do".

Item	Alternatives	Ranking
16.1	What do you prefer, me always telling you what to do, or you finding out for yourself?	
16.2	If I keep coming up with the answers, and it keeps not working, where do you think that leaves me?	
16.3	Alright, I want you to get moving and do what you are paid to do.	

Situation 17: When you ask the salesperson what the goal is, they say "I have to reach target, don't I?".

Item	Alternatives	Ranking
17.1	That's up to you is not it?	
17.2	Not really. It's what you have to do, but sometimes it might not be your personal goal.	
17.3	Is reaching the target your goal?	

Situation 18: You ask the salesperson what help they want. They cannot think of anything.

Item	Alternatives	Ranking
18.1	What about me coming out with you?	
18.2	Does that mean you can perform to standard without help?	
18.3	If you want, I can make some suggestions.	

Situation 19: The salesperson says all the right things, but you still feel uneasy, and their performance never improves.

Item	Alternatives	Ranking
19.1	I have to say that I feel uncomfortable with your behaviour. You say the right things, however, you do not appear to implement any plans we agree.	
19.2	I do not believe you.	
19.3	If you are doing all the right things, why is it that your performance never improves?	

Situation 20: This is now the last chance. Your boss has given you a deadline either to improve the salesperson's performance or to get rid of them. During the coaching session, the salesperson says they will take a particular course of action. They have never kept to any previous commitment.

Item	Alternatives	Ranking
20.1	Look, this is the last chance. If you do not get it right this time you are out.	
20.2	What has happened in the past when we have agreed this course of action?	
20.3	I am under pressure from my boss to get rid of you, so it better work this time.	

Score Sheet — Put your ranking against the item number

Item	Rank	Item	Rank	Item	Rank
1.3		1.1		1.2	
2.1		2.2		2.3	
3.3		3.1		3.2	
4.3		4.1		4.2	
5.1		5.2		5.3	
6.1		6.2		6.3	
7.1		7.2		7.3	
8.3		8.2		8.1	
9.1		9.2		9.3	
10.3		10.2		10.1	
11.1		11.3		11.2	
12.2		12.3		12.1	
13.3		13.1		13.2	
14.1		14.3		14.2	
15.1		15.3		15.2	
16.1		16.2		16.3	
17.3		17.1		17.2	
18.3		18.2		18.1	
19.1		19.3		19.2	
20.2		20.1		20.3	
Total 'A'		Total 'B'		Total 'C'	

FEEDBACK ON PROFILE

An average profile would be a score of 34 in 'A', 37 in 'B', and 49 in 'C'.

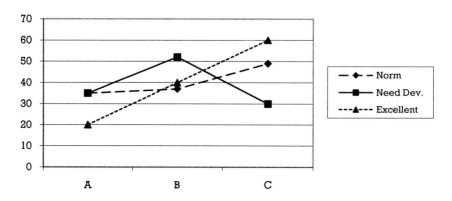

Figure 13: Feedback on Profile as a Coach

If you have a score of between 31 and 40 in column 'A', you have a good grasp of coaching principles and the model.

A score of between 20 and 30 in 'A' would show a remarkable theoretical ability. I say theoretical because, as in all things to do with skill acquisition, the proof of the pudding is in the application.

If your score in 'A' is in the range 41 to 60, then you still have some way to go. You need to consider how much you stick to being in control, and whether you are able to empower people yet — keep with it.

The only relevant scores are those in column 'A'. Scores in 'B' and 'C' merely indicate that further consideration needs to be given to your initial response.

CHAPTER 6
A SYSTEMATIC APPROACH TO SALES COACHING

Well done is better than well said. Benjamin Franklin

SALES COACHING IS NOT JUST A TECHNIQUE

Many managers attend courses to learn sales coaching skills, believing that sales coaching is a technique that can be implemented in any organisation. My belief, borne out by experience, is that some organisations are not geared up to take advantage of the opportunities that sales coaching provides for performance improvement. In many ways, sales coaching is more of a cultural issue than a technique. Coaching requires foundations to have been laid before coaching begins. There are rules for successful coaching.

There are two main ways in which to approach sales coaching. Each depends upon the culture of the organisation and the needs of individuals and organisations. Each also depends on whether the sales coach is a line manager in an organisation seeking to improve the performance of a team, or whether the coach is acting as an external coach seeking to improve the performance of a particular individual. In both cases, it needs to be established whether the coach is working to a set of rules that have been established already by the organisation or whether they are seeking to find the drivers of performance from a particular individual or team. Three routes are shown here, although there are probably many variants.[21]

---

[21] Such as those organisations using self-employed salespeople or agents to sell their products and services.

COLLECTIVE APPROACH

The collective approach (**Figure 14**) requires the coach to determine the rules and to implement them.

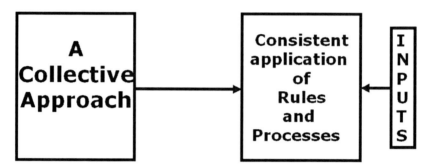

Figure 14: The Collective Approach

The sales coach knows what works and performers have to learn to play by the coach's rules. The only time that the performer can negotiate a different approach is when they are operating above the current minimum standard. For most of the time, the coach should feel in control. The only occasion when the coach begins to question this route is when they encounter resistance from 'star' performers who baulk at the 'straitjacket' approach that this route feels like to them.

This approach is particularly effective in organisations where the sales coach is the line manager, and there are a number of people reporting to the line manager who have similar or the same roles. This is especially so if the coach or the organisation has designed a process that they want the team or a number of teams to implement in a consistent manner either within a defined department or across a geographic area – e.g. there is a branch network where the company requires or wishes the service to customers to be the same no matter where the branch is located.

The collective approach is focused on inputs.

THE INDIVIDUAL APPROACH

The individual approach allows the performer to determine the rules. In this example, the sales coach and/or the organisation is unsure of what works and how sales success is achieved – other than by such non-specific elements as commitment, determination, hard work, or even personality and positive attitude.

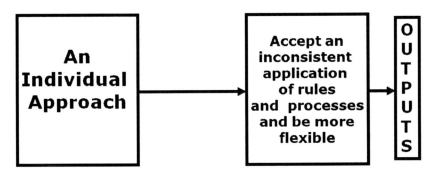

Figure 15: The Individual Approach

There may be individuals who are performing well, but they are not keen on letting the line manager get close to them. The sales manager thus allows the salesperson a lot of space.

The individual approach might be applicable in an organisation where there are specialist jobs; where numbers carrying out the role are small. The individual approach is often the only way in which an external sales coach can operate – unless they have been provided with a specific set of rules the organisation wishes to implement.

The individual approach is focused on outputs.

Whichever route you choose, both eventually end up at the same point – implementation of rules. Having said that, there is another route.

THE ENTREPRENEURIAL APPROACH

The entrepreneurial approach is similar to the individual approach in one respect – there is a lot of flexibility, but it goes beyond flexibility. It relies upon individuals who have their own way of doing things. The organisation allows the individual total freedom, and the salesperson plays the game according to their own rules. In reality, the people who operate successfully in these environments have no rules other than 'This is the way I do things. You can take it or leave it'.

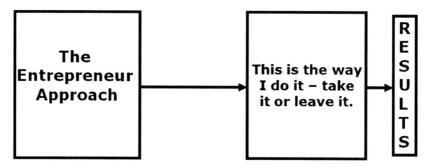

Figure 16: The Entrepreneurial Approach

This is not a route for the faint-hearted manager or coach, especially if you are the line manager. In many ways, you need to adopt a *laissez faire* attitude – but, if this happens, then you need to question what it is you are there to do.

On the other hand, as an external coach, perhaps this is the approach to take – there is only so much you can do as an outsider without line authority. There are no controls. For significant periods of time, performance is high, however each success can be tinged with a few problems, which inevitably you as a sales manager may end up sorting out on behalf of the performer. You do this willingly at first because sales results are coming in. The only time that problems exceed results is when the performer moves on to pastures new. It is likely that not all of the problems created by this *laissez faire* attitude come out of the woodwork during the tenure of the high performer. Sometimes the trading practices of salespeople allowed to operate in this environment can leave much to be desired.

External coaches operating in this mode also can find it frustrating. The point of sales coaching is to see improvement. Without some form of commitment to buy into the process, improvement can be spasmodic.

EFFECTIVE SALES COACHING RELIES ON PROCESS

There is a significant difference between using a sales coaching model (such as GROW or POWER©) and applying a systematic approach to the holistic view of sales coaching. Sales coaching does not sit within a vacuum and cannot work in isolation.

It has not been unusual for me to be approached by a company and to be asked to train their sales managers in sales coaching technique. Though painful experience, I have learned first to investigate whether the training will work. It really is pointless training managers to be sales coaches if the environment in which they operate almost guarantees that they will not succeed.

For one thing, what exactly is it that the sales coach will be expected to improve? It is not possible to improve sales performance without considering what it is the salesperson is expected to do. It is this lack of focus that I found in many sales organisations and which makes a lot of sales training and sales management training a complete waste of time, money, and resources.

In sports, coaches and players follow structured processes. The players know what to do, how to do it, and when to do it. The coach gets the players to practice the process and then to improve the process. They do not make it up as they go along. It is exactly the same in the other professions I have already mentioned: music, dance and acting. In sales, all too often, when you ask the salesperson what is to happen at a customer meeting, they respond "We'll play it by ear".

A HOLISTIC MODEL FOR THE COLLECTIVE APPROACH

The following holistic model to sales coaching, when implemented properly, is guaranteed to work. This particular model is focussed on the collective approach. It begins with process and comprises nine elements:

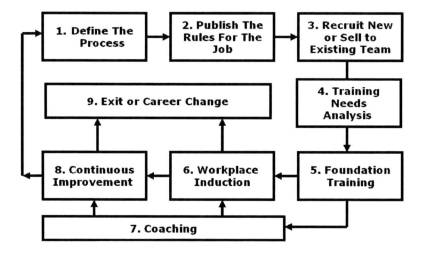

Figure 17: The Collective Approach – A Holistic Model

1. What is it that needs to be done and how is it to be done? The sales coach has to be able to draw this out and understand clearly how a task is to be performed. They may observe existing successful salespeople to determine how sales success is achieved or, if there are no success stories, they may buy in or copy a successful sales process from an external source. The difference between this approach and life skills coaching is that life skills coaching requires the person being coached to determine the agenda, whereas this approach focuses on the agenda dictated by the business.

2. The second part of this approach is concerned with clearly establishing the rules of behaviour. Following process definition, the rules of how to perform the job role should be published. It

needs to be made clear to the sales performer what is expected of the role and, just as importantly, how the role is to be performed within a set of parameters determined by the business.

3. The third task is concerned with either finding people to match the profile of someone you want to carry out this role or selling the profile to the existing team. In an ideal world, it would be great to start with a new team – in truth, this is not realistic. Unless a business is in start-up mode, the luxury of starting afresh is not available. Sales coaches have to contend with resistance to coaching as a concept at work and, in addition, a population who may not be ideally suited to the process you want to implement. The optimum place to establish acceptance or resistance of the rules surrounding the job role is at recruitment stage, but the coach may have to undertake a considerable effort to sell a new process to a sceptical existing audience.

4. From this, you determine what training is to be delivered. You also may have to alter your views regarding the level of training required based upon the available candidates applying for the job. Whatever the situation – you need to conduct a training needs analysis. You cannot coach people unless they have been trained. Sales coaching is about improvement – so therefore you need a foundation upon which to build improvement.

5. The fifth element of this holistic approach is to design and implement a foundation training programme that provides the new performer with a set of basic skills and knowledge required to fulfil the job role. Even if staff already are *in situ*, that does not stop you from establishing new criteria for future recruitment and selection and, in time, by implementing the sales coaching process, the current population will become up-skilled to the levels of a future desired intake.

Sales coaches also understand that, although the performer may be experienced, they need to attend foundation training. The experience they bring with them, whilst relevant and pertinent in previous organisations, most likely will need to be adjusted to fit in with the new organisation. Many sales organisations make the mistake of believing that, by employing successful salespeople from competitors, they have negated the need to invest in foundation training. Sometimes, it works – but, quite often, it does not.

6. The sixth and seventh elements are concerned with ensuring that the training moves from simulation and theory into reality. This is where sales coaching begins and, at this level, coaching is about ensuring that what has been learned on a training event – either on a formal course or through one-to-one skills drilling – is transferred to the workplace. Induction happens in the workplace. Workplace induction is the acid test of whether theory matches reality.

   The coach has to work closely with the trainer to agree a) criteria for learning objectives on the foundation programme and b) how to transfer these to the workplace. In organisations that have centralised training facilities, it will be possible to design an exclusively workplace-orientated foundation and induction process, something which is covered later during this programme.

7. The first role of the sales coach is to implement foundation training by checking whether the performer has acquired the agreed levels of knowledge and skills during foundation training, and whether they can display the attitude desired of effective performers.

   Coaches begin by checking out that training has worked. They establish what the individual has learned and test it. They establish what the skill should be and check it out in simulation. Then they observe the execution of that skill in 'real time'. Last, they check that the trainee is adopting the right attitude with regard to implementing the training. The coach cannot move onto element 8 – improvement, if the trainee is resisting change or simply cannot, or will not, implement the new skill or knowledge.

8. The ultimate aim of the coach is to improve performance. Training teaches basic skills. Coaching exceeds basic performance. Only when the first seven processes have been completed is it possible to focus on improving performance. The coach needs a platform upon which to build a robust performance improvement plan. We teach people to do the job; we coach them to excel at it.

9. Within this holistic approach, there may be times when the new or existing salesperson can, and should, exit the cycle. For example, if they do not accept the rules or they do not want to engage in the process, or they fail basic training, or they cannot transfer learning to the workplace or, more positively, if they outgrow the current job and want to and are able to move on.

In an organisation that already has people *in situ* (which will be the majority), despite perhaps not wishing to put everyone through a re-selection process, the coach nevertheless needs to establish whether the performer accepts the job role. For new starters and new roles, the best time to test performers will be at recruitment and selection. For existing performers, resistance to either new job functions or roles will come out during the workplace coaching process.

For others, it may become obvious during the foundation training period or at workplace implementation that the individual may not be suitable to continue with the organisation. It is better to tackle this immediately rather than let the situation fester.

Last, a consequence of performance improvement for some people is that they grow out of the current role and the coach has to accept that a percentage of people will outgrow his or her involvement. In some cases, the performer needs a new coach to take them to a higher level. In other cases, they need a new job. The coach should welcome the realisation that their influence has developed someone to the extent that they no longer need them. This is a major difference between the attitude of professional coaches and some traditional managers.

A HOLISTIC MODEL FOR THE INDIVIDUAL AND ENTREPRENEUR APPROACHES

Using a similar model to the collective approach, the following is focused on the salesperson. It also tends to be the model used in personal coaching.

In this instance, the coach either has no line authority or suppresses line authority. Perhaps he/she is operating as an external coach. In either case, there are eight elements in the process:

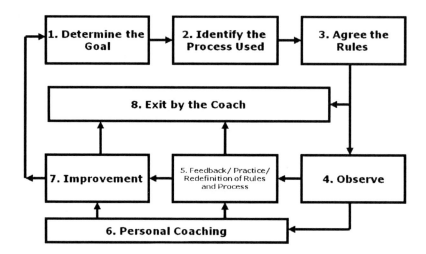

Figure 18: The Individual and Entrepreneurial Approaches – A Holistic Model

1. The first task is to establish the overall goal and whether that goal is realistic within the time-frame. The sales coach expresses their own goal first – which is to establish a desire to help the individual improve their performance in a given task, or in the undertaking of a specific process. They then discuss with the individual what they are expecting to get out of the coaching relationship and determine what success will look like

2. The second task for both parties is to identify the process. Every job function has a process attached to it – e.g., this is how the job is done. That is not to say that all jobs have been critically analysed in this way, and it could be that this process alone – determining in detail how the job is carried out – has enormous benefits for the performer. Certainly, the coach needs to know what it is the performer is trying to achieve within a given process.

3. The third element is concerned with establishing the rules of engagement. The coach needs to explain in detail how they will work with the performer, how long it might take and what has to happen. For example, the coach must be able to see the performer in action at some stage, otherwise the discussions and the coaching sessions only ever will be seen from the performer's perspective. For example, if the coach is working with a salesperson who is experiencing difficulties with someone else, and it has been agreed that the salesperson will discuss with that person the issue in a certain way, or adopt a certain new behaviour, the salesperson may come back to the coach and say "I did what we agreed and it did not work". There is only one way in which to guarantee that what has been agreed is implemented and this is through observation.

4. Thus, the fourth element of the process is that coaches must observe performance. There is no other way. How to set this up is explained elsewhere but, for the purpose of this section, let us make it absolutely clear that coaches have to observe performance in 'real time'.

5. At the fifth stage, coaches provide feedback. This may also result in a redefinition of the process(es) that are seen to work or not work, and may also require redefining the rules.

6. This is where coaching begins and where it is most effective. But, without going through the previous stages, coaching will not result in improved performance.

7. Having determined the goal, identified the process, agreed the rules, observed performance and provided feedback, the coach is able to improve the performance of the individual by focusing on one piece at a time (whole-part-whole – see **Figure 10**).

8. As with the collective approach, there are a number of exit points, this time for the sales coach. If the sales coach and the salesperson are unable to determine or reach agreement on the goal, or the goal is unrealistic within the time-frame; if it becomes impossible to define a process, usually because the salesperson does not want to go through the process, which can be lengthy; or the salesperson and the sales coach cannot agree the rules of

engagement; or the salesperson will not allow the sales coach to observe them; or the salesperson reacts badly to feedback; or there is no improvement; or improvement has reached the stage where the sales coach believes that the salesperson would now benefit from engaging another sales coach to take them to another level; then the sales coach should withdraw. Sales coaches also must understand their own limits.

Chapter 7
PURPOSE AND PARAMETERS

The very essence of all power lies in getting the other person to participate. Zig Ziglar

I developed the POWER© model of coaching in 1993, soon after attending *The Challenge of Excellence* course run by David Hemery and Susan Kaye. It is a further extension of the model used by Hemery and others called GROW (which stands for Goal, Realism, Opportunity, and Want). David Whitaker said that "GROW is a checklist that helps me stay on track". In the same way that I believe in a structured approach to the sales process, I welcome all models that keep coaches on track and help the salespeople to focus on achieving a result.

The POWER© model of coaching evolved from working with sales managers, salespeople and the successful application of the coaching process I have been involved over a period of 20 years. It should be noted that it also has broader application for any business manager.

POWER stands for:

- Purpose and Parameters.
- Objectives and Options.
- What's happening now?
- Empowerment.
- Review.

The POWER© model is a tool that can help sales coaches to practise in a very focused way what is often called MBWA — management by walking around. POWER requires the sales manager acting in a coaching capacity to get involved with the sales team. Leave your desk and go into the field where your sales team are plying their trade. Be available to performers, observe, ask questions, listen and discuss performance. Catch people doing things right and also highlight areas where improvements are required. POWER will assist you to get results through your sales team in a structured fashion over time.

I have worked with many sales managers who think they know how their salespeople operate but confess after a field coaching session that they had never prioritised the observation, analysis and feedback of their sales team before. Comments like "I was really shocked when I spent some time with John and saw how weak his sales skills are" or "I now know why Mary is successful but there were still opportunities for her to cross-sell more" are commonplace. The reality for many sales managers I have worked with is that, because they are busy with so many administrative tasks, sometimes they find they have been concentrating on the wrong activities. Even when sales managers are out with their sales teams in the field, they often are unsure how to maximise their one-to-one time with them. POWER will assist the sales manager to get results throughout the whole team.

The model begins with setting the agenda and reviewing the journey towards excellence thus far. The key to sales coaching is goal-setting. Second, assess whether the aims and objectives of the performer are in line with those of the sales coach and the organisation. The third stage is about understanding whose actions have brought about the current results — this is where the focus moves strongly into personal responsibility. The fourth stage is about taking that responsibility for making things happen, for making improvements, and for contracting with the coach to work on an improvement plan. The final stage is about analysing the results and making plans for the next stage of improvement.

I use the word 'power' in a positive sense. I see power as being the life force that exists in most salespeople and something that can be translated into constructive endeavour. I see sales coaching as returning power to individuals. The problem is that we enter the world powerless and, whilst the possibilities open to us are endless, the realisation of those opportunities heavily relies on being given power by others in order to act. In the processes of growing, learning, and being cared for, ruled, controlled or directed, that return of our personal power or empowerment sometimes can fail to emerge. The more civilised the society, the greater the number of rules. We began with Ten Commandments and now we appear to follow several million laws. It seems that the longer we exist, the more we rely on telling other people what to do. It is small wonder that people have lost the ability to think for themselves and, more importantly, act for themselves. I tend to agree with Samuel Smiles,[22] who in 1859 said:

> Whatever is done for men or classes, to a certain extent takes away the stimulus and necessity for doing for themselves; and where men are subjected to over-guidance and over-government, the inevitable tendency is to render them comparatively helpless.

In essence, the more you do for people, the less they are able to do for themselves. The mantle of personal responsibility is a difficult one for sales managers to shed, yet to get the best out of people, that is exactly what you have to do.

Using the POWER© model as a framework, coaching becomes a series of structured questions in which the salesperson increasingly takes the initiative in setting and achieving goals. The model is simple to remember and, with practice, can be delivered in an easy, conversational style. That ease of delivery belies the powerful nature of its potential impact.

PURPOSE AND PARAMETERS

The first part of the model is concerned with defining the purpose of the coaching session and the parameters to be agreed upon. That is to say, what is it possible to achieve within the time available? Most people go straight into defining objectives and, from my experience, it is in the lack of clarification of the purpose and parameters of the coaching sessions that many sales managers and salespeople can stumble at the first hurdle. Having an unclear purpose for the sales

---

[22] Samuel Smiles, *Self Help*, Penguin, 1986.

coaching session even before defining goals is like flying off into the fog and then later deciding on a destination. In any case, the process of questioning the purpose of the session in itself prepares salespeople to take part psychologically in what is to come. As the sales coach, ask yourself what you want from the session and how reasonable it is. How much time do you have and what exactly are you trying to achieve? Is there something that you are working on for the whole team or is this session part of an overall plan for an individual?

All too often, I have seen business coaches and sales trainers allow the salesperson to set the main agenda for the coaching session. I believe it is the sales coach's responsibility to keep the coaching sessions focused on business issues. That is not to say that the coaching sessions exclude any personal development; however, personal development needs to be addressed within the context of what the organisation is trying to achieve. This is where sales coaching and counselling are a million miles away from each other.

In counselling, the person being counselled sets the agenda and the timescale is as long as someone is prepared to pay for the counsellor's time. In sales coaching, the purpose is about improving performance within a realistic timescale and some financial boundaries. It is pointless coaching an individual who is taking too long to respond. The set parameters should have an eye on the clock and the calendar.

If I were a sports coach, I might see a dramatic improvement in a runner's time over 100 metres. However, if I gauge that, at the current rate of improvement, it will take three years to reach a qualifying time for the Olympics and the games are two years away, then what is the point? The point might be that I make the runner a better person and help them achieve their personal goals, but then that is not what I am being paid for. I am being paid to help the athlete win medals. I have to understand what the organisation wants. If the organisation is satisfied that we perform better than we did in the last Olympics, then well and good. I might be able to accommodate the performer within a team effort. The result may be a better international standing. The point is that I need to establish what the rules are at the outset. I need either to agree with the rules or find another game to play. I need to communicate the rules and my expectations at every opportunity, and certainly as part of each coaching session.

The purpose and parameters part of the POWER© model is where you establish and reinforce the mission of the organisation and the vision of you and your team. It should be the starting point for all coaching sessions and all contact with the team. As a sales coach, ask yourself these questions often:

- Is what I am doing leading me towards my goals and vision?
- Are my goals and vision aligned with those of the organisation?
- Are the salesperson's goals aligned with the team vision?
- Are the salesperson's goals aligned with the organisation's vision?

It is pointless working at something that the organisation neither wants nor recognises. There must be a return from your investment in coaching for the organisation as well as for the individual. Often, I have found that sales managers, in particular, are so busy building internal empires that the corporate goal gets lost somewhere.

For sales managers, it sometimes appears that achieving targets is the sole mission statement. This is a very important area for sales managers and requires closer examination.

TARGETS

There are two types of targets most often associated with selling and sales coaching:

- Financial targets, i.e. results.
- Activity targets.

So where do they both fit into the system?

Financial Targets: Results

You may believe that financial targets belong in the rules section of the professional processes or the holistic model. Whilst understandable from one perspective, placing financial targets amongst the rules can cause problems.

If I am a footballer, I understand the rules of the game and must follow them, but nowhere in the rules does it say that you must win. The purpose is to win, but the rules do not say you must win. It is accepted that it is pointless playing without the intention of winning; however, winning is something that is not necessarily within my control. If my colleagues and I play well and to our potential, if we score more goals than the opposition, or let in fewer goals than the opposition, we will win. But what if they play better? What if the referee makes a series of bad decisions that go against us? Winning is a purpose, the objective, the goal, but it is not a rule. I do understand, however, that there are consequences in not winning, and I understand that, if we do not win, then we will not qualify to play in Europe. We may be demoted. I may be transferred. Even so, winning is not part of the rules.

So how can meeting financial targets in selling be part of the rules? There are benefits and consequences. Some of the benefits are that, when I make my sales targets, I might qualify for an incentive scheme and feature in favourable sales dispatches in my region. If I do not meet the financial target, I will lose my job. It is unlikely the sales manager will lose their job, unless they consistently and repeatedly fail. As a salesperson, I do not get too many chances.

The principles that apply to the other professions should apply to here too. Clearly, there have to be benefits and consequences, but consequences are not the primary focus. To get the best out of an individual, as a coach I have to focus the individual on delivering a professional performance. I cannot have the performer worrying about the big picture. That is part of my accountability, even though the consequences of non-achievement also will affect the performer. They know what they must do and they understand the consequence of failure but, in order to deliver their best, they must focus on what they are doing, not on the long-term goal.

I am not saying that you hide the desired end result or ignore it. It must be part of the focus every now and then. You must check whether people are moving forward and whether there is a likelihood that the end goal eventually will be achieved, but you must get the performer focused on the job in hand every day, not on the journey's end.

One thing you must do, however, is to make it clear from the outset what the long-term goals are and the consequences of non-achievement. These have to be set out very clearly at recruitment stage. You tell people what is expected, the benefits of the job and outline the consequences of non-achievement. You would be wise also to say how you are going to help them achieve the target and what training and support they will get. You should encourage them by telling them how many people are successfully achieving the target and how long it took them to do so. And therein lies a problem.

I have come across a significant number of sales forces in which over 70 per cent of the individuals are not achieving target. In these circumstances, it makes it even more critical that targets are not included in the rules, yet my experience shows that they usually are. The rationale is that because somebody is achieving and even exceeding target, then anybody can. There are two issues at work here:

- You need to be sure that it is possible for all of your sales team to achieve target, given the variables of market size, population distribution, and competition.

- You need to know in some detail what it is that those top performers are doing and how long it took them to achieve target.

From the latter information, you formulate the rules of the game and invoke basic training to replicate what it is they do. At recruitment stage, you explain how top performers are achieving target and therefore what you will be teaching the new starter and what is expected of them in terms of following the rules of the game.

Activity Targets

Given the choice between buying an activity management system and implementing a performance coaching system to bring out the best in salespeople, my unfortunate experience is that many senior management teams inevitably choose activity management. The reason? It's easy. OK, so you have to push people around a little, and you might have to dismiss a few non-achievers but it is a relatively easy thing to implement and to control. Yet my firm conviction is that it is easy because it does not work. It works in the short term, granted, and there is even a place for it during field induction and as a mechanism for performers to appraise themselves, but as a coaching tool, it is a non-starter.

I believe that you teach salespeople about activity, not force it on them. If you teach by example that activity is important, that is quite different from demanding levels of activity. The danger with the latter is that your salespeople deliver the activity without a corresponding increase in business. I have numerous examples of salespeople forging activity levels simply to keep the sales manager happy. In the meantime, the hoodwinked manager sinks into a quicksand of statistics trying to work out where it went wrong.

I recall visiting an area sales manager who was having problems with a non-performing salesman. When I entered the manager's office, there was a mountain of paper on his desk. He proceeded to tell me about Jack Newton, who was under-performing and had been doing so for some while. He told me that he had insisted that Jack increase his customer interviews from eight per week to 20 per week. The manager showed me the charts he had put together showing the pattern of calls and results. When he opened it up, it filled the surface of the desk in front of me. It was very impressive. It must have taken him quite some time to put together. Jack was now calling an average of 21 customers per week, but his results had not increased.

I arranged to meet Jack with his manager present and I asked Jack to bring his diary. When we met, I opened Jack's diary and I pointed to the first name entered on Monday morning. I said, "Jack, if I ring this person up, will he know who you are?". Jack looked in pain. "Yes, of course", he said. I said, "Jack, if I call all of these people, will they all confirm they know you?". Jack paused. "Yes", he said. "Jack. I'm going to ask you one more time, just to save me the trouble of telephoning all of these people, which is what I intend to do. How many of the names in this week of your diary will confirm that they have met you?". Jack paused for longer than he had before. "Most of them", he said. "But not all of them", I said. "No", he replied. Out of the corner of my eye, I could see the manager sinking into the furnishing of his chair. "Jack", I said slowly, "this is now really the last time I'm going to ask you. When I call all of these people, how many will confirm that you have been to see them, that you attempted to sell them your service, that they were not a personal friend?".

Over a couple of months, Jack had falsified 80 per cent of his activity. He was responsible, but it was not his fault entirely. The manager had forced him to achieve an arbitrary activity target and had abdicated his personal responsibility of spending a few days with Jack showing him that activity mattered but that it is not the only thing that matters. Seeing more people is too easy a remedy.

ABOVE AND BELOW THE LINE

There is a distinction between what your role has to be with new starters and with experienced salespeople, and whether they are overachieving or not. The principle is that you train and manage people up to the line, and you coach people above the line (**Figure 19**). Up to the line is where you set your benchmark – the basic minimum requirement.

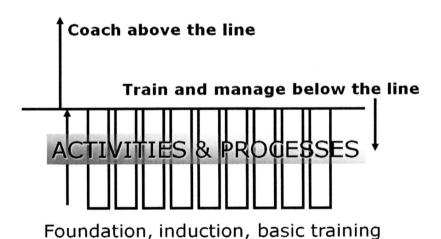

Figure 19: Above and Below the Line

Above the line is where you seek to help people excel at the job. You cannot help people to excel at the job until they reach the line. Below the line are your minimum expectations, the elements that include the requirement to learn a sales structure, knowledge levels or procedures.

Below the line is where you apply the rules. There is no negotiation below the line. You make it clear what is expected and you implement it. These are the rules that are spelled out at recruitment. You make it clear what will happen when someone starts in your team. You do this before they join the company, not after. All too often, I have met salespeople on induction training courses whose idea of what the job entailed and reality were miles apart. You must make it absolutely clear what you expect them to do and how you expect them to do it.

You may produce figures that show that, from a particular level of activity, a particular financial outcome is being achieved within the salesforce or that the relationship between activity and income leads you to believe that the more people you see, the higher the potential results. You may choose to ignore the fact that top salespeople see fewer customers than their lower-performing colleagues. Nevertheless, you need to ask yourself what you want from the salesperson. Is it activity or results? Forget the relationship between activity and performance — do you want activity or results? If it is results, then apply the rationale we have laid out in detail above. If it is activity, then perhaps you have lost the plot. The most important thing to you as a sales manager and a sales coach is results and your job as a coach and a trainer is to improve on performance. Anybody can increase activity, which is but a measure of performance. If performance is low, one of the elements of increasing it can be increased activity – the easiest way in which to increase performance by playing the numbers game.

That is not to say that you cannot influence activity, but it is not coaching, it is training. Part of the central training programme could, and should, contain basic training on the activities that go towards making up the prospecting part of the sales job. It is right to expect that people work hard in return for what you pay them, but that is a philosophy that new people will learn from what they see about them. The greatest influence on that will be you and the rest of the sales team. The greatest influence on the rest of your sales team is you.

TESTING

You influence people about activity by making sure that you reinforce the central training. You do this by meeting the new starter immediately after the training programme. Your job is to check that they have accepted the philosophy of the company (which could include work ethic), that they have acquired whatever level of knowledge was expected (so you test it), and that they have acquired the expected skill level, which means that you test it in role-play.

These are the important tests before you allow the salesperson in front of a customer. As a precursor to this, you have to be 100 per cent confident that the central training process works and that the format of the central training programme delivers to you exactly what was agreed. Otherwise, when someone starts with you in the field and they either do not accept the company's philosophy about work ethics or have not acquired the level of knowledge and skill you expected, then you will not be able to decide whether it is the new starter's fault or the central training department's fault.

I suggest you sort all this out long before you start employing salespeople. You and the training department must have complete faith in each other's ability to deliver exactly what has been specified.

The last part of this phase is that you must accompany the new salesperson on a live customer call. It is the only way in which to ensure the transfer of theory from the recruitment stage and of basic training on the central programme to where it really counts, and that is in front of the customer. There is not a professional coach alive who does not sit on the touchline, stand in the wings, sit in the auditorium, or watch the actual performance as part of their coaching responsibilities.

There is nothing you can do about the performance except learn. Part of the purpose and parameters of a coaching session with a new starter should be to check that the new starter has arrived in the field with the knowledge, skills and attitudes you expected.

You cannot coach new starters until you satisfy yourself that all of the elements contained in basic training have been mastered. If you do try and move ahead in one area while leaving another basic element incomplete, you will find that the foundation stones of performance are not strong enough to support the effort needed by both you and the performer to improve. Be careful about coaching an improvement in one area while gaps appear in the basics (**Figure 20**).

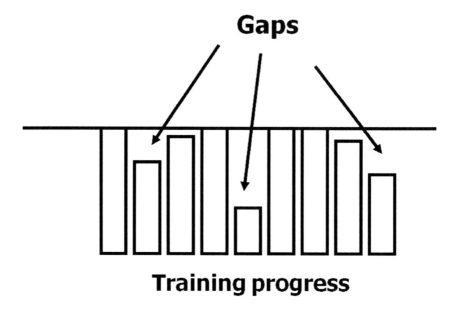

Figure 20: Avoid Gaps in the Training Process

My recommendation is that you should accompany the new starter in the field for five days after the central training event. You will come up with all sorts of excuses why this cannot happen and these excuses will compromise the successful outcome of both training and coaching. All too often, I see examples of sales managers having high hopes of new starters only to dismiss them a few months down the road. What happens to all the positive expectations sales managers have of new recruits?

The highest level of labour turnover in sales forces happens in the first six months of a new salesperson starting. In many cases, I have observed managers extending probationary periods because they were unsure whether the new person would make it. "I'm giving him one last chance to prove that he can make it" is an often-heard comment. What about giving yourself one last opportunity to get it right? If you have made the right decision at recruitment, then there should be no reason why every new starter cannot succeed at the job.

Think about it. It is probably not a complicated job to do. You will have done it. Others are doing it. So what is it that happens to so many new starters? The reason is you. Unless you meet people on day one in the field, test that they have acquired the levels of knowledge, skills, and attitudes required, accompany them immediately on a real sales call, and stay with them for their first five days in the field, you will have to rely on luck as to whether new starters make it or not.

It is during these first five days in the field that you teach new starters the activity game. Ideally, you will already have arranged a number of sales appointments for the first week. Otherwise, how will you observe a live call? It is no good leaving the new starter to fend for themselves. No matter how confident they are or are supposed to be, remember what it is like starting in a new company. It can be demoralising to realise that the big talk on the central training course was simply that — big talk, no action. How many training courses have you been on where the only thing you are asked when you get back to work is, "How did it go then?", followed quickly by, "Oh well, back to work" with the underlying message that whatever happened on the course is not the same as real life — and the tragedy is that it is probably a correct assumption.

What happens on central training courses has to reflect down to the last detail what happens in the field. There can be no compromise, no negotiation. There is no negotiation on activity up to the line. After salespeople have reached the line, then they can negotiate about activity, but do not be confused between work activities and call activity. What you want are people to have the right work ethic. You want them to work hard. You want them to perform. You know that you cannot perform without hard work. Sure, there are a very small percentage of people who seem to be able to perform without a lot of hard work, but they represent less than one per cent of the sales population, and the chances are it is more perception than reality. It is well expressed in the old adage that success is one per cent inspiration and 99 per cent perspiration!

The level of activity you want for a new starter begins with what you show them in the first five days of field induction. The central training programme is the foundation; induction happens in the field. If you believe that salespeople should be making 10 calls a week, then arrange 10 appointments for the first week. Either you do it or integrate it as part of the central training programme. If they are learning to make telephone calls on the central training programme, you could incorporate some reality into it by having them make live calls and appointments for the week they are with you in the field.

In the first five days, you will learn more about the new starter and they will learn more about you and your company than through any other mechanism we know. You must know within those first five days whether the new starter will make it or not. If after five days you still do not know, then chances are they will not make it and you should let them go. However, you also should conduct a full review of why it happened this way. There is no guarantee that every new starter will succeed, but you substantially reduce the risk by operating the system we have just described.

If someone does not work out during this period, you must analyse what went wrong and patch up any gaps or failings in the system. Recruitment, training, and field induction are too expensive for you and the company not to take it seriously. I know of many companies where a proper professional approach to the recruitment, selection, foundation training, and field induction of the type I propose here would add five to 10 per cent profit to the bottom line.

Whilst you are operating below the line, the way in which you deal with low results, accompanied by low activity, is not to instigate minimum activity levels — I have already covered the dangers of this. That is not to say you ignore it, but to move from a training role to a coaching role, you have to get the salesperson to accept personal responsibility for their activity and for their results.

Have the new starter collect and collate their activities for a specific period and have them agree that, whatever that level and quality of activity is, it has an outcome – it produces a certain level and quality of results. If that level and quality of results is below your benchmark or minimum standard, then you move onto getting the new starter to face the question, "What if we need this level and quality of results?". What you want people to take responsibility for is that their actions produce their results, and that these are below what was expected or agreed. Say something like "At the time, we agreed that this is what you would do and achieve, that this is what is expected of you, that this is how we play the game in this company, and that this is the level and quality of support you can expect from me. What we have is a shortfall. It is now your responsibility to alter the outcome by altering the input".

In this way, the new starter has a choice: either they improve the quality of their business or they increase the amount of activity that gets them appointments. In reality, if you have any sense at all, you want the first option, but you will accept the second option. The choice, however, has to be theirs.

You may refer to the first week in the field. You may cite the level of work you were both involved in during that week, but never fall into the trap of accepting responsibility for coming up with the answers to low performance, otherwise you will teach the new starter that the responsibility for success and failure lies with you, not them. If you insist on call activity levels, then do not be surprised if they come back to you and say "I'm now doing more calls but not more business. What do you suggest now?". It is this sort of mistake that causes most sales managers to suffer the stress levels I see as normal in the profession. I cannot say that professional coaches do not suffer from stress, but it is different to the stress suffered by many sales managers.

Now for the £1 million question — what would you do if you had set call activity levels of 10 calls a week, and a top performer consistently only delivers six calls a week? When I have posed this question to groups of sales managers, they split 50 per cent, 40 per cent, and 10 per cent. Fifty per cent say they would leave the over-performer alone, and not discuss the shortfall on activity. In fact, they admit that they would spend as little time as possible with the over-performer for fear of upsetting them. In doing so, they miss out on all of the untapped potential of top performers who operate without a coach. Forty per cent usually cannot make their minds up, relying on whoever spoke last to agree with. Ten per cent get aggressive about the lack of activity, and complain, strut and posture, but do little other than make sarcastic remarks to the salesperson, ensuring that they move on to another company at some stage.

The answer? It comes back to what you taught them in the first five days of their field induction. If you taught them the work ethic, then you still can work on helping them to deliver a full day's work for a full day's pay. You shouldn't put it like that, but you live the philosophy of 'nobody's so good they cannot get better'. All top performers in all other professions have the desire to improve, and have the coach work with them. It is only in sales that top performers resist the sales manager's involvement.

When Steve Redgrave, surely the greatest Olympian of modern times, made his acceptance speech for BBC Sports Personality of the Year 2000, he mentioned four people. Three of them were coaches; the last was his colleague Matthew Pinsent. The problem is that I know of no salesforce that has a raft of different coaches working with salespeople at different stages in their careers. Redgrave changed coaches as he got better. Each coach worked at a particular level of performance, each knew the limitations of their coaching ability to get the best out of Redgrave, and he knew it also. They were not in competition with each other; they worked together to release the potential that Redgrave had. That is an important point to remember: do not foster competition internally. Redgrave was not in competition with others in the boats he rowed in — he was in competition with other boats. Internal competition is destructive. Have your salespeople compete with the competition, not with each other. You want them to help each other, not try to get one over each other. This can be difficult to achieve in practice and is dependent on the organisational culture to some extent. However, in my experience, once again it is the sales manager who will set the values for the team. The best coaches help performers to play to their strengths and recognise and help overcome obstacles. They foster real teamwork. Champion coaches recognise that, as in sport, the biggest challenge sometimes is inside one's own head.

Once the salesperson has hit the benchmark level of performance — the minimum standard – the emphasis is to move the performance slightly forward. It does not have to be by much, but one of the major rules of your coaching regime should be that 'We are here to improve, not to stand still'. Whatever we do, we get better. The aim is to get the performer to accept personal responsibility for improving, whether they are on target or not. In fact, the target becomes irrelevant. You cannot improve someone's performance whilst concentrating on the target. The only way to improve performance is to concentrate on making a step forward — by improving how they do something.

It is important to give the performer emotional strength through your support and your expectation of success. You need to transfer your positive expectations about the potential of the performer to them: "I know that you can perform to a higher level. I know that you can be even more successful". But be careful about expectations that are set too high, too quick. One step at a time is enough.

SOME QUESTIONS TO ASK

How much time do we have? The response to this question should be followed by the coach establishing what is feasible within the timescale. For example, you could begin: "Obviously, 30 minutes will only allow us to get a feel of what we are trying to help you achieve, and it's highly likely that we may have to schedule a further time slot soon to take this initial discussion a stage further. Are you comfortable with that?".

If it is a later coaching session, where some work has already been achieved, then both coach and performer will have become used to establishing the parameters relating to time. Be careful if, through familiarity with any or all parts of the process, you become tempted to skip parts of it, assuming that the performer knows the rules of the game. It is always dangerous to assume and the fundamental precept is that ideally each part of the process should be adhered to on each occasion.

Use the term 'we' whenever possible. Much of the coaching session is a shared responsibility. The only time that using 'we' is inappropriate is at the point where the salesperson has to do something. 'Doing' is the salesperson's responsibility. Later in the model, when action is being sought, it would be inappropriate for the coach to say: "What are we going to do now?". At that stage, once action has been agreed, it would be a case of: "What are you going to do now?"

What is the purpose of this session for you? The salesperson must articulate the purpose of the session. That said, if the salesperson comes up with a purpose that the coach does not feel would add value to the salesperson's performance, the validity of the salesperson's choice can be questioned. For example, you could ask: "How will this add value to your overall performance?". Having received a reply to this, however, the coach then should back off. By pushing, the coach may intimidate the salesperson into saying exactly what the coach wants to hear. Coaching technique can be manipulative in the wrong hands. Manipulation merely results in the coach's aims and objectives being realised, and whilst salespeople may enjoy short-term benefit, it is rarely sustainable. Classically, the charismatic trainer will elicit commitment during a training event, which eventually is weakened by the passage of time.

What are you looking for from me? The coach needs to establish from the salesperson what they believe the relationship is to be. I have already said that the relationship is different from that of client and counsellor. Somewhere along the line, the coach may direct – and not necessarily with kid gloves. Coaches have objectives to achieve, too.

If what is expected from the sales coach is thought to be unreasonable, say, within the timescale, then the coach is entitled to say so. All matters of a performance nature come from the salesperson. The sales coach may very well be a major influence, but performance comes from within. The sales coach may motivate, but the salesperson may remain unmotivated. Some coaches have unrealistically high expectations of their powers of persuasion.

These sessions, whether they are at the beginning of a sales coaching programme or represent an element in the middle or at the end, are central to the success of coaching. Get this wrong, and it will all go wrong. More time should be spent defining the relationship and establishing goals than in coaching itself.

GUIDELINES FOR COACHING SESSIONS

It is important that your first face-to-face sales coaching session with your sales performer is handled well. Organise it as you would any other business meeting by indicating the purpose and benefit for the salesperson. For example, you could say: "Let's get together to review how your sales figures for last month have gone. We can focus on any lessons that will help you to achieve your half-year sales figures target".

To help you prepare, you could script your opening sentences. Practise beforehand, as you should for any important meeting. Ensure that the session:

- Is in private.
- Is not interrupted (switch phones to voicemail).
- Has been allocated sufficient time to produce a meaningful meeting. Do not extend it beyond two hours maximum. Otherwise, fatigue will set in and diminishing returns will result.

You should also ensure that:

- You are well prepared.
- The salesperson is receptive to the meeting.
- You have a coaching notepad to record issues discussed.
- The salesperson also has a notepad or coaching log to record issues or action points that arise.
- There is not a third party present, or if there is, that you focus on the salesperson during the meeting.

COACHING TIME

One of the common criticisms of coaching is that managers often say that they do not have enough time to coach. In my experience, sales managers who successfully coach find it indispensable and argue the opposite — you do not have time *not* to coach.

One bank manager I worked with, who embraced the coaching process, described his situation:

We needed to appoint a new sales co-ordinator. Now I spend half an hour a week with this individual, looking at issues, discussing job needs and agreeing a structure. It is the individual who must appreciate the importance of this coaching. I realise that some company managers would say they do not have the time to spend helping staff in this way. But if I can get people to a certain standard, we can divide the workload and make it easier to achieve our objectives.[23]

Coaching does not have to be a full day with an individual. It can last five minutes, half an hour, an hour. It can span a week, a month, six months or a year. It will depend on the overall purpose, the coaching relationship, progress made and the coaching agreement itself.

In my experience, sales coaching should represent 60 per cent of the sales manager's available time. This is a challenging figure for some, but coaching can achieve sales results that make the investment in time worthwhile. In my experience, the coaching relationship should receive as high a priority as other business activities. It involves discipline on the coach's part to manage time and to prioritise the coaching sessions. Consider arranging to meet once a fortnight. Once you agree a time slot, manage your schedule to ensure it happens.

In committing to the coaching agreement with salespeople, the sales coach needs to commit more than time to ensure success. As a sales coach, your behaviour must be supportive of the process. For example, if you take issue with your salesperson's late arrival for meetings, ensure that your timekeeping is better. Similarly, if you talk about the need for your team to demonstrate loyalty and dedication to the organisation, ensure that your own behaviour does not demonstrate lack of loyalty and dedication. Otherwise, your team will have difficulty in differentiating between what is actually important and what you only say is important. If there is any doubt, your team will place more emphasis on your behaviour than on anything you say to them.

---

[23] 'First National: Getting it all Together', *Sunday Business Post*, Excellence Through People supplement, 14 December 1997.

As a sales coach, you must abide by rules, too. Demonstrate genuine commitment to the coaching purpose. In this way, your behaviour will directly and positively influence your sales team's behaviour and commitment to coaching.

CHAPTER 8
OBJECTIVES AND OPTIONS

*The key to productive goal-setting is in estimating clearly
defined goals, writing them down and then focusing on
them several times a day with words, pictures and
emotions as if we have already achieved them.*
Dr Denis Waitley

Some people advocate that coaching should begin with the performer setting out their goals and objectives. The coach's job then is to help the performer achieve those goals and objectives. But what if the goals have little or nothing to do with what the company is trying to achieve? What if the objectives fall short of the target? It is an area that you will have to give a considerable amount of consideration to. However, my stance is that the performer should be given the opportunity to set his or her own objectives within the business parameters you have set. The parameters as outlined earlier in this book must be in line with your sales team's vision and that of your organisation.

Sales coaching is not life skills coaching. You are not responsible for providing the salesperson with a ticket to a happy and fulfilling life. I believe that the coach's involvement in helping salespeople to achieve their potential will have many positive benefits. However, I do not believe that it is essential in sales coaching to provide people with a set of skills applicable to ensuring a rich vein of life and interpersonal skills. That said, your own goal here is to attempt to have the salesperson align their goals and objectives with those of the company. However, you also should be aware that, at the outset, it is vital that you have set your own goals. This will, and should, form part of your vision, which the salesperson has to be encouraged to share. This is not as difficult as it may seem. Research into the subject of charismatic leadership[24] shows that many followers are ready and willing to buy into the goals of leaders, even subjugating their own previous goals in order to help charismatic leaders achieve their goals. I am not advocating that you have to be particularly charismatic in order to have your sales team buy into your vision, goals, and company objectives, but you do have to work on your own skills and ability to communicate effectively with the team and the individuals in it.

What I already know is that 95 per cent of the population have no goals other than to be happy, healthy, and wealthy. Surprisingly, in my dealing with many salespeople working in teams, I have seen scant existence of any specific goals, timescales, or indeed any plans to achieve goals other than some vague ideas about working hard. Yet goal-setting is an integral part of sales coaching.

An inability to clarify goals and objectives is like having an open lifetime journey ticket and leaving the destination up to the driver, whilst you, the passenger, sit passively in the back seat. People spend considerably more time planning their holidays than they spend planning their lives. Defining objectives is of equal importance, whether for the complete coaching programme, in terms of current work or of long-term goals. Each leads to the next and is reliant upon getting the first step right. The identification of objectives and options locks into that primal need for achievement, to know that we are progressing toward something and not just aimlessly drifting.

Does the sales coach require any special skills in setting goals? Yes, if you are trying to set goals that motivate. Goals that are either too difficult or too easy actually can de-motivate. If a goal is too difficult, a person either may give up right away, realising the goal is unattainable, or become frustrated in a vain attempt to reach an unreachable goal. If a goal is too easy, then a person does not feel challenged or stretched, which is what McGregor's Theory X and Y is all about. Building on Theory Y, we know that people actually want to achieve more and to improve their performance. The challenge for

---

[24] R.J. House, *A 1976 Theory of Charismatic Leadership*, Southern Illinois University Press, 1977.

the sales coach is to set goals that can be achieved, given the resources available to the individual.

BEGIN WITH THE END IN MIND

In Stephen Covey's best-selling book, *Seven Habits of Highly Effective People*, he reminds us that physical creation begins as a mental creation — as a thought, a plan, a perception, or a motive. He believes that one of the most powerful habits of successful people is 'to begin with the end in mind'. In other words, we cannot be successful if we do not know where we are going. He comments that every successful action in fact has been created twice: first in the mind, in how we envision our success, and then secondly in the physical production of desired results. Like most good pieces of advice, it is a 'BGO' — a blinding glimpse of the obvious. However, commonsense is not always common practice.

Thus, we need to create our results mentally before we can create them physically. Take the example of a forthcoming sales presentation to a new client. If you know what you want to accomplish at the meeting, you can define its purpose. The coaching encounter focuses on the mental creation, the envisioning of a particular result, which precedes the physical creation – the physical production of desired results.

INTERIM AND END GOALS

Is it a good idea to 'begin with the end in mind' at every coaching session? Should we remind ourselves that we are trying to achieve the 'four-minute mile' or should we just focus on the immediate tasks of the training regime? Working backward from the end goal can be more motivating because the person being coached can visualise clearly the success. In sports, a coach needs to be able to focus the athlete's attention on the big picture, while also motivating them to do the training and preparation. There are milestones along the way and the immediate focus is the short-term or interim goal. The end goal is akin to the well-known analogy about the elephant, which can only be eaten in bite-sized chunks. There will be many meals before the elephant is finally eaten!

The same holds true in business, where the goals are about skills that have a physical and mental dimension. The end goal defines the route that must be taken towards the finishing line, but it should not be the focus of each coaching session.

As covered in **Chapter 4** (view of a traditional sales manager *versus* the sales manager as sales coach), some managers concentrate too much on the end result or are obsessed so much with 'what-ifs' that they fail to start off right, and subsequently fail to complete a task effectively. All sorts of jobs suffer from the 'running before walking' syndrome; it is all part of the 'I want it, and I want it now' culture. The sales coach's role is not to slow down progress but to ensure that progress is maintained towards an end goal.

While the coach has their eye on the end goal all the time, that is the coach's job, not the salesperson's. This becomes the relationship between the salesperson and the coach. The coach holds the end goal on behalf of the salesperson, yet it still belongs to the salesperson. It is like depositing a goal into a performance bank, where the coach is the cashier. Every now and then, the coach lets the salesperson know how much interest has accrued, and how far it is to the end goal. The salesperson at any time may change the end goal – that is not the coach's choice. The coach merely keeps the salesperson on track and informed. In the working environment, therefore, the relationship is the same. With the help of the coach, people decide what they want to do and how they intend to achieve it, in steps from the immediate to the long term.

Defining the immediate objective before beginning is vital. Most people have some idea what the long-term, or even medium-term, goal is. What they have problems with is with the immediate goal. Each journey begins with the first step. That first step leads to another, and eventually the destination. The beauty of taking things one step at a time, however, is that, with each success along the journey, the eventual destination also moves, and goals become more and more ambitious. In any event, the journey for many people is just as rewarding as the destination.

The coach's job is to help to define the immediate objective and desired outcome of the coaching session, and then to break that down into its component parts. This may take time, and indeed, if done properly, it should. It should never be taken for granted that the salesperson understands the objective of the session, and the coach must not be intimidated by the exasperation of the salesperson as that immediate objective is sought. The important thing at all times is that the coach and salesperson have to build a trusting relationship which allows each to express themselves freely. If the salesperson has difficulty in determining the immediate goal, the coach should be able to say: "The worst thing here would be for me to suggest a goal for you. It's a sure-fire recipe for you to feel disappointed if you achieve it because it wasn't your goal, and for me to feel disappointed if you do not".

Let's look at a musical analogy. When taking trumpet lessons, Karl O'Connor (one of the authors of the first edition of this book) went to a music coach in the symphony orchestra. Before playing a note, the coach focused him on what his end goal was — whether to play the trumpet professionally or as an amateur, and to what standard of performance. Having agreed that the end goal was to play solo as an amateur in a brass band, the coach then helped him to identify the immediate objective of the first class. What scales had to be played and to what standard or grade did an agreed piece of music have to be performed? The journey then began. Both parties knew what the end goal was but the focus became each class with accompanying short-term goals.

HOW TO SET GOOD COACHING GOALS

Goals should be specific and measurable. They should have a time-scale. Vague goals cannot produce optimal results, because they do not specify what optimal means. The following are examples of vague goals:

- Provide excellent customer service.
- Increase sales by as much as possible.
- Improve relations with our customers.

These goals cannot be acted upon, nor can they be measured. Let's look at revising the goals to make them usable:

- **Vague:** Provide excellent customer service.
- **Specific:** Set up a customer help line by the end of the quarter.
- **Vague:** Increase sales by as much as possible.
- **Specific:** Increase year-on-year sales by 15 per cent.

To be actionable, a goal must be specific and measurable. What gets measured gets done. In this regard, the sales manager acting as sales coach should inspect what they expect from the performer, for example, by accompanying them regularly on customer visits.

THE GOAL-SETTING PROCESS

Different organisations set goals in different ways. Quite often, the sales manager does not have huge room for manoeuvre in terms of annual and interim targets, which often come from the top. However, given that as a sales coach you will be setting both performance and behavioural goals, you are likely to have three types of goals:

- Top-down goals and objectives.
- Collaborative goals and objectives.
- Bottom-up goals and objectives.

As sales are ultimately what make an organisation profitable or unprofitable, sales targets tend to be set at a very high level within the organisation. Other goals simply must be met — for example, compliance with new regulations relating to data protection. It is likely, therefore, that the sales manager as coach must bring certain pre-set goals to the coaching session. However, how these goals should be achieved must be discussed between the coach and team. Even if you have top-down goals, it is important that you discuss the goals and explain why it is important to meet those goals. If you adopt a take-it-or-leave-it approach, you are likely to build up resistance. It is better to have a discussion about the impact of top-down goals and examine the set of tasks that must be undertaken to achieve them.

In one organisation I worked with, this is exactly what happened where the head of sales presented the sales goals as a *fait accompli* and refused to discuss them with his sales managers. This led to hostility and a belief on the part of his sales team that the goals were unattainable. The goals subsequently were not achieved. The following year, the head of sales was replaced by someone who involved the sales team more in agreeing stretching goals. There was greater buy-in as a result and higher motivation on the sales team's part to achieve the goals. The sales performance improved following this consultative process.

Collaborative or participative goals are very important to the coaching process. If you constantly impose top-down goals, you will find it difficult to encourage your team to identify and take ownership of those goals, because they do not see them as their personal goals. As I mentioned earlier, when people have an opportunity to set their own goals, they often set targets that are higher than those set by the company. Not only that, but because they identify with those goals, they tend to have a greater chance of achieving them.

Where goals relate to behaviour, it is very important that there be a collaborative process in setting those goals. To change behaviour, the performer needs to have a very high level of self-awareness about their current behaviour and have the desire and commitment to change to a more positive behaviour. Remember, it is very difficult to change behaviour. You must first unlearn what you have been doing wrong, and that takes time and effort. Then the new behaviour needs to be practised for so long that it becomes 'second nature' — that is, an unconscious competence.

Bottom-up goals, where the performer sets out personal goals and objectives that they want to achieve through the coaching process, can help you as coach to get more buy-in on the performer's part. While any goals must fit in with the organisation's objectives, you may find that the salesperson suggests developmental goals that you had not considered but which contribute to the well-being of the salesperson and the organisation as a whole.

SINGLE FOCUS

One of the things I have learned about professionals in sports and the performing arts is the existence of what is termed 'single focus', which is the ability and strength to be able to block out everything else and concentrate on what it is you are attempting to achieve in any particular moment. Dave Lakhani[25] calls it *Fearsome focus*™, which he says is the single-minded ability to concentrate fully on the task at hand without allowing anything to impact the effort to perform that task.

Lakhani uses a 45/15 formula, which means that, for salespeople, the focus of activities for 45 minutes in any given hour should be on the things that will result in sales – such as prospecting, or talking to customers. The other things that take up a salesperson's time, such as driving, answering emails, research, should take up no more than 15 minutes of every hour – if that. Sales coaches also must be aware of, by analysis, what it is that salespeople do that brings about a sale, and delegate non-sales influencing tasks to others.

GOOD COACHING QUESTIONS TO ASK

For new starters:

- Having completed your induction training and as part of your field sales work, what do you think we should be working on next?
- How will that help to get us on target?
- What else could you do?
- How will that work?
- Where do you think we should be up to by now?

For those performing below the acceptable performance line:

- What do you think we should be working on now?
- How will that get you back on track?
- How long do you think that will take?

---

[25] Dave Lakhani, *How to Sell When Nobody's Buying (And How to Sell Even More When They Are)*, John Wiley & Sons, Inc., 2009.

- What else could you do?
- How will that work?
- What help do you need?
- What will be the return on the investment?
- How will this contribute to the overall aims we have?

With an over-the-line performer, your aim is to raise their expectations and to have them committed to improvement. For this reason, you need to adopt a far more democratic style in setting the objectives. We already know that, by adopting the 'whole-part-whole' approach, any item within the job specification or job profile that is improved will increase performance.

You can use the Performance Wheels (**Figure 21**) to help both you and the salesperson focus on what you should work on. Simply draw two circles on two separate sheets of paper. Using the first — positive outcomes — ask the salesperson, "What do you do that you believe makes a positive contribution to your performance?". Check out each item by asking, "How does that work?". You need to keep asking this for clarification until such time as you believe you have items that you could help them improve on and which you could use to train other salespeople. Quite often, top performers have ideas about their performance based more upon myth than fact. Many simply do not know what it is that contributes to their performance. This type of questioning helps them to focus on practical, skills-oriented elements rather than attitudinal elements, which are difficult to train or coach. Then ask, "What help do you want from me to tackle one of these items?".

With the second sheet — negatives outcomes — simply ask, "What do you do that you believe detracts from your performance or that you believe you could do better?". Then, "What help do you want from me to tackle one of these items?".

Contributes to: -

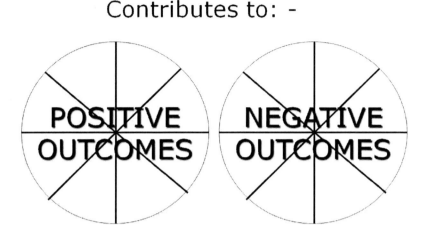

Figure 21: The Performance Wheels

ADDITIONAL QUESTIONS FOR EVERYONE

What are you trying to achieve? It may take some time to establish the real goal. It could even be that the salesperson has no clear idea of what they are trying to achieve. In work environments, it can be usual for individuals not to have clear personal goals. The organisation may or may not set out its corporate mission, or the sales department may or may not have quality standards or a shared vision. For the coach, sometimes getting the salesperson to identify the existence of a personal goal can be a frustrating search.

As I have already said, we are very used to being told what, when, where, and how to do things. Faced with the opportunity to determine our own strategy for life, it is hardly surprising that most people do not know where to start, and indeed fail to see why they should.

Do you see this as a company goal or your goal? Even when the organisation or the sales director or sales manager sets goals, it is important to achieve organisational goals willingly. The practice of resistance becomes so innate that we also end up resisting our own development sometimes. If the salesperson feels that the goals are set by someone else, then you should ask:

How can you make it your goal? It is important that the individual takes personal ownership of any objective. It is pointless continuing the coaching session if the salesperson persists in saying that they have no choice in determining the goal. In some cases, the salesperson may say that their goal is to achieve the company target, which is fine, provided that they accept the fact that they have a choice whether to perform or not. There are obviously benefits in achieving company targets and consequences in not performing to the company standard, but the choice we all have still remains a personal decision.

As their line manager and coach, it is best to focus on motivating the salesperson by focusing on the benefits to them of achieving the goal. In this regard, you should match the rewards for accomplishing this goal to their own tangible and intangible needs. By 'tangible', I mean rewards of a material nature that are directly linked to their jobs, such as salary and fringe benefits. Intangible needs are more personal or psychological, such as the need for security, social belonging, esteem, independence and self-realisation. As their coach, the more you know about the salesperson's tangible and intangible needs, the better you will be at motivating them. In order to help them see the benefits of adopting a sales goal, you could ask them to outline the benefits of attaining it. For example: "Michael, if you realise this goal, what are you going to get out of it?".

It is far better for the salesperson to set a personal objective that is below the target than to blindly accept a given target which they personally believe is not achievable.

Is this the whole goal, or is it part of something more long term that you want to achieve? The purpose of this question is to help the salesperson begin to focus on the first step. While it is essential to 'begin with the end in mind', you will not achieve that end if that is all you think about. Unless followed up immediately with physical action, mental commitment always will remain a thought and not a reality.

The planting of a number of seeds also safeguards against crop failure. Often the people who are the most disappointed in their career are those who failed to reach a single, specific goal. It did not materialise and, without it, came failure, despondency, or embitterment. The journey towards goal achievement calls into a lot of different ports on the way. Life is about experience. We are who we are because of our past, and we will be who we want to be by the actions we employ now and in the future.

Sustainable goal achievement is a result of constantly moving the long-term goal. Therefore, as coach, you need to probe the salesperson's attitude towards goal achievement.

Visualise yourself achieving your goal. Now describe what you will feel like when you achieve your goal. All motivation is internal. It may have external influences, but the drive comes from within. These prompts focus on the internal drive. They also seek to create a picture of achievement. As I said, success is created twice, once in one's 'mind's eye' and then again in reality. The coach should encourage the salesperson to visualise success and to feel the elation of achievement. For example, in a sport such as golf, a player can visualise putting his ball into the hole as part of his preparation on the golf green. The player should see the ball drop in his mind's eye and feel in advance the sense of satisfaction on holing the putt.

Is there anything else that you could do? Is the identified goal really it, or has its identification been more to do with the pressure of the coach? Has the identification of the goal been clearly thought through? Is there something else that should be on the table? It could be that, beneath the surface, another goal — the true goal — lies hidden. The coach should help the salesperson investigate as many options as the salesperson can think of. Some of these, whilst not immediately desirable as an alternative or even realistic for the moment, may provide choices for a later stage in the process.

Goal-setting is not about identifying the one goal. Putting all your faith and energy into just one goal can be dangerous. One of the goals has to be the major goal, the one that consumes most of the salesperson's early effort, but we all need a fallback position if something goes wrong. That does not mean that we have a lack of commitment, or positive attitude. Positive attitude and commitment however, are simply not enough. There are some people who pin all their hopes on achieving one goal and believe that a positive attitude will make things happen, when to an onlooker it is patently clear that they are overreaching themselves.

You may be totally committed to winning the 100 metres gold medal, and have a tremendous positive attitude about the reality of winning it. It may have been your lifetime goal. On the day, what happens if the person next to you runs their lifetime best and beats you? We all have to live with ourselves after the event. Having options, planting seeds, and developing new goals all helps. It does not make the commitment any less significant. It is not defeatist, it is coping.

People do, however, have to decide for themselves what the alternatives are. It is common at this juncture for the salesperson to ask the coach what they think, and perhaps to come up with some alternatives. It is also common for the sales manager or the trainer to then respond. After all, it is quite flattering to be asked for advice. Most people, when asked for advice, will give it. There is a danger in responding too early, though. Have you ever given some advice to someone only to have them respond, "Oh, I tried that, and it did not work"?

The chances are that, if the individual did not come up with the objective or alternative themselves, the lack of commitment will contribute to failure, thereby reinforcing what a bad idea it was in the first place. Most salespeople fail to reach company targets not because they are unachievable, but because they have not accepted them. The same is true of options. The coach can contribute to the generation of options, but only if the parameters have been set first: "I've got some ideas and some options that you might want to consider, but I stress that they are my ideas. They might not work for you, but if you want to hear them, I can share them with you. The important thing is that I'm not recommending any one. The decision as to their acceptability still rests with you".

Which course of action do you favour? What are your reasons for choosing this approach? This is to help the salesperson decide which is the most favoured course of action and to become aware of why they have chosen this approach. The coach has to be non-judgemental. Whatever the salesperson decides is right, even if it is wrong. By returning to this whole process time and time again, the salesperson will work out for themselves what was right and what was wrong, and what worked and what did not. You may feel that this might take forever and, in the early days, it may seem as though it does. However, like the tortoise and the hare, the best route is not necessarily the fastest.

As with the previous question, the generation of choice is a matter for the salesperson, not the coach. It is also remarkable to observe, no matter how experienced the coach may be in the completion of the task, how different people find different ways of completing the task, each of them as successful as the other. Having trained someone to do the basic job to standard, then growth above the line will be achieved only when the individual is able to express themselves in the work arena in the way in which they feel most comfortable.

The trainer and the sales manager will help the individual to learn the basics, explain the procedures, and give them induction training to do the standard job. To excel at work, however, the performer needs to be determined, with your help, to improve. What you are looking for are the answers to performance improvement that might be beyond your own experience or even capability. You need over-performers to experiment in order to find out what could work and what you could teach to others.

When do you want to achieve this goal by? It is easy enough to talk about having a goal, but the true measure of commitment to achieve it is determined by setting a deadline. Whilst the coach may be leading the salesperson to give a commitment, the salesperson sets the time. The coach needs to be able to make an assessment of the potential work involved in helping the salesperson achieve their goal, and to establish whether it is realistic. Even so, the answer to realism lies with the salesperson, and hence the importance of the next question.

How realistic is that? Here is an opportunity for the salesperson to think again about the realism of committing to a specific time. From experience, the coach may know how realistic the timescale is, but it is not for them to comment unless asked. The worst thing a coach can say, and this applies to any stage of the process, is: "Well, in my opinion ...".

These two questions related to time and schedules conclude the goal-setting aspect of the model and represent the cornerstone of coaching principles. The failure to achieve worthwhile goals has little to do with ability, but rather has more to do with a lack of vision and planning. The difficulty most of us face is that simply reading the questions to yourself does not seem to work. It is their articulation that adds weight and, eventually, action. As with most goal-setting activity, people rarely write their goals down, specify exactly what they mean by them, or set timescales. We all know the theory. The practice, however, is seldom achieved alone.

Herein lies the importance of the coach as a catalyst in the process. The mere fact that an external source asks the questions appears to bring about a positive series of actions. People are at their best when they have someone they feel attached to and who they feel can help them.

> Human beings of all ages are happiest and able to deploy their talents to the best advantage when they are confident that, standing behind them, there are one or more trusted persons who will come to their aid should difficulties arise. The person trusted, also known as an attachment figure, can be considered as providing ... a secure base from which to operate.[26]

Now immersed in the model, it is worth noting that the elements contained therein, whilst initially following a predestined course, can and often do retrace steps when one element proves difficult to establish. It would be quite usual for a question such as 'How realistic is that?' to call into doubt the original goal, timescale, or even relationship of coach and salesperson.

Remember, too, that the coach will have goals. Being a sales coach is not a vocation, and sales coaches do not have to sacrifice their own career, aspirations, or even integrity for the greater glory of the performer. At some point, the coach may decide that the goals, action plans, and deadlines are so unrealistic as to warrant a withdrawal. That is not to say that the salesperson may not achieve their goal eventually either alone or with another coach. Also, within work environments, the physical withdrawal of the coach may not be possible or even allowable. But I use the word 'withdrawal' in the

---

[26] John Bowlby, *Attachment and Loss*, Harmondsworth, Penguin, 1973.

emotional rather than the physical sense. I proposed earlier how the coach might tackle their return to a more traditional managerial role, rather than that of the coach. The decision as to which game is played rests with the salesperson.

In order to help the sales coach set the ground rules for the coaching sessions, I have drawn on a sporting analogy with regard to the use of yellow cards and red cards.

YELLOW CARDS AND RED CARDS

You may have heard the term 'three strikes and you are out' from baseball, or be familiar with the yellow card, then red card, scenario in football. Whatever the analogy, there have to be penalties when coaching someone, especially with regard to the rules surrounding activity between coaching sessions.

Presumably, you will set an agreed action plan for the two of you to tackle between the current visit and the next. The sales coach may have to do something, and the salesperson most certainly will. The first thing that the sales coach does on the following visit is to check on what the salesperson has done. It is important to keep fastidious notes, both about discussions and observations. If you have more than one person to coach it can be difficult, without good note-taking, to recall what happened last time.

The important thing for the coach is to take a view on whether the salesperson has worked on the action plan between visits. If not, you give the first warning. It is time to show the yellow card, which will alert the salesperson to the need to mend their ways: "OK, you say you have not had time. Whether you have or not is a matter for you, but what we now have is that my time is being wasted. I cannot move forward with you unless you practise/implement what has been agreed. What you need to do for next time is [whatever was supposed to have been done]. Let's recap what the benefits were for you in doing this. When I see you next time, I expect this to have been completed".

When you meet with the salesperson next time, you check whether the task has been performed or not. If not, call it a day by using your red card: "It was clear last time we met that I did not enjoy wasting valuable time. You missed an opportunity the last time; you are missing another opportunity this time. I could have helped you as I've helped others. It's time to call it a day on coaching, as you have not played your part as agreed".

GOALS *VERSUS* OBJECTIVES

I've written a lot about goals in this section. Is there a difference between goals and objectives? Essentially not, other than objectives in the POWER© model always should come down eventually to a short timescale. Whilst some goals may be long-term, all objectives of coaching sessions should be for short-term implementation; therefore, they need to be short-term objectives. It is important for the sales coach to agree on the implementation of actions that will be implemented now – not some time in the future. The longer you leave it between agreeing an action to be undertaken and the actual objective to be achieved, the more likely it is that it will not happen.

CHAPTER 9

WHAT IS HAPPENING NOW?

We chose to go to the moon in this decade, and do the other things, not because they are easy but because they are hard. J.F. Kennedy

We have now reached the very heart of the coaching process. We have already looked at the purpose and the parameters that guide the overall coaching relationship and set out the rules and roles for the sales coach and salesperson in each of the coaching sessions. We have also looked at what the salesperson wishes to achieve through the coaching intervention. Now it is time to look at the current situation. This is a vital part of the process. 'What is happening now?' is reality. Salespeople need to face reality and, in essence, that is what true sales coaching is primarily about — sales coaches put salespeople in touch with reality. The purpose is to make salespeople understand that their current behaviour and efforts are producing their current performance. Put simply, what you do determines what you get in return. Clearly, if the salesperson wants to change their current performance, then they must change their current behaviours. It is all too common for salespeople to blame others and the general situation for a lack of performance. 'What is happening now?' is meant to establish the fact that each person ultimately is responsible for themselves. In this chapter, I look at a key coaching technique, observation, which you can use to get a realistic, unbiased view of the current performance. With this point in mind, I focus now on what happens during a field coaching session.

FIELD VISITS

For line sales managers, the most important area of work they undertake is in time spent in the field with their sales teams. The sales manager's primary area of responsibility lies in coaching salespeople. It is through the continual on-the-job development of front-line salespeople that the company will achieve its objectives. All other things being equal, it is the effectiveness of salespeople that will ensure continued success.

New starters usually attend some form of training event on joining the company, either delivered centrally or in the branch. Whilst containing some or all of the skill elements necessary for sales success, as highlighted previously, there is no substitute for field training and coaching by the line manager. In fact, within 24 hours, line managers either build upon the work done centrally or jeopardise the frail foundations put in place. For many salespeople, the content of most sales training events represents theory. What the manager says in the field is reality. If the manager reinforces what happens on the course by employing the same processes on the job, then training will become a reality. If the manager either debunks the central process or fails to observe the salesperson immediately in the field following training, then the initial training investment will be wasted.

THE PURPOSE OF FIELD VISITS

In client companies with which I have worked, when questioned about the purpose of coaching and observation field visits, sales managers have come up with the following:

- To provide appraisal evidence.
- To improve performance.
- Checking up.
- Compliance.
- Increased sales.
- Motivation.
- Training.

When salespeople in these same companies were questioned about the purpose of coaching and observation visits, they came up with a different list:

- Checking up on me.
- A free lunch.
- Keeping in touch.
- I need help.
- I need to prove that low performance is not my fault.
- Something for the manager to do.
- I have no idea.

Thus, right at the outset there can be differing views. Coaches should ask themselves this question when determining the purpose of the coaching and observation visit: "Will the individual be a more effective, better-motivated, and more professional salesperson as a result of the time invested with me?".

This question encompasses a number of elements:

- **Individuals:** Each person has a unique style and delivery. Whilst at the outset, we may be prescriptive in the sales process adopted, each person eventually will deliver a performance that is unique to them. Coaching, in contrast to training, recognises the individuality of each performer.
- **More effective:** The primary task of a line manager is to help the salesperson to improve results, preferably by coaching. The sales coaching visit is an opportunity to build a stronger relationship with the salesperson, who in some instances may have more specialist skills than the line manager.
- **Better motivated:** Some people say that managers can provide only a motivational environment and that all motivation is self-motivation. This fails to recognise that managers play a vital part not just in maintaining a motivational environment, but sometimes also by leading from the front. People can be motivated by the behaviour of the manager, just as they can be de-motivated by managerial behaviour. Managers make a significant difference to the performance of their teams. Time and again, it has been

proven that manager behaviour begets the behaviour of their direct reports.

- **Professional:** Line management's responsibility is to ensure that a quality service is provided that adheres to internal as well as external policies and procedures. A primary function of the coaching visit is to confirm that salespeople comply with the legislative requirements that may be placed upon the company by the relevant regulator or by internal procedures.

- **Time invested:** Management time does not come cheap. Time is money, but like all investments, there is no quick return. Granted, there is a pressure to get people up and running quickly; however, we also know that the best results from salespeople are achieved by way of tenure as well as effort. The longer successful salespeople stay with us, the more they produce. The quality time spent with salespeople developing their individual skills through coaching is the most productive time a manager can spend. No amount of meetings and training sessions can substitute for coaching visits.

A FRAMEWORK FOR FIELD VISITS

The coaching and observation visit is a four-part process:

- Preparation.
- Observation.
- Discussion.
- Consolidation.

Preparation

Before conducting a coaching visit, managers need to prepare themselves, prepare the salesperson, and prepare for each coaching observation.

Personal Preparation

Each manager should keep a log of coaching activity carried out with their salespeople. For example, in determining what a salesperson's training needs are, it seems unlikely that coaches will remember what was discussed on the last coaching visit. What happened and what development and improvements were agreed upon should be recorded.

Coaches should be clear about their own objectives. What are you trying to achieve? How long have you got? Is it reasonable to cover the objectives in the time allotted?

If the salesperson is under-performing, are you aware of any personal problems that may be getting in the way? Selling is a stressful occupation and the existence of personal internal pressure is common enough. People who have problems outside of work generally bring their baggage with them when performing the job. If the sales job is all about commitment, motivation and communication, then personal problems can affect performance. How close are you to your team? Do you know them well enough to know when something is going wrong outside of work that may be contributing to what is going wrong at work?

Have you thought about the benefit to the salesperson of your visit? How will you agree it, and how do you intend to express it? Like everybody else, the salesperson constantly asks themselves WIIFM — what's in it for me?

What about arranging a coaching visit where the salesperson is making a sales presentation? Is it something you do on the spur of the moment or is it a regular arrangement? Both have advantages and disadvantages. One of the problems with arranging coaching visits too far in advance is that the salesperson fixes up an ideal day, unless they are trying to make a particular point about poor business conditions. If you have built up a trusting relationship with the salesperson based upon the POWER© coaching principles, then there should be no problem in turning up either at short notice or without notice. Remember, your objective is to observe the salesperson in their natural environment. If you arrange the day and specify the number and type of interviews, the chances are that (a) it just will not happen that way and, consequently, you will be displeased and the salesperson will be under pressure from the word go, or (b) they do what you want, simply to return to the old way of doing things when you have gone.

Preparing the Salesperson

Ask the salesperson to consider their own strengths and weaknesses. What do they want to do better, and what do they want to do less of? Help the salesperson to focus on positive behaviours and eradicate negative behaviours.

Do you have a measure of the salesperson's ability? If you do not, how will you know whether they are getting better or worse? It is easy to measure results, but often it is too late to do anything about them. Far better to measure processes that contribute to results. You can do something about processes; you can do very little about results. Results are something that has happened — like a company's balance sheet, they are history. Once sales opportunities have been missed, they stay missed. Unless you get salespeople to adopt positive processes, they will miss similar opportunities when you are not with them.

Are you aware of the personal interests of the salesperson? What makes them tick, and what is there about the rewards of a successful performance that can help individuals achieve their personal goals? People do not work simply for money, although we recognise that money can be a prime motivator for many salespeople. Salespeople also want recognition for a job well done, and a sense of achievement. When top performers were asked what their main motivation was, they said: "Doing what's right for the customer and doing a good job". If they did this, they reasoned, they would reap the rewards. Nobody would argue with that.

Is the salesperson aware of the company's aims and objectives? Too often, staff surveys uncover that people are totally oblivious to the company's aims and objectives. It is not that they are not interested; it is that nobody keeps them involved. If people are not made aware of the direction of the company, it is likely that they will be going in the opposite direction, or eventually leave to find a company they feel more a part of. People want to be involved. In one company, top salespeople bemoaned the fact that they were selling low-profit products but only received the management information at the end of the sales year, when it was too late. If they had been kept in the communications loop from the start, they could have been selling a better class of product to customers, which was also more profitable from the company's perspective.

Preparation for Each Observation

What are you going to focus on in the call? The first time you may observe the whole performance, but when it comes to deciding what to improve, you can only tackle one thing at a time. Many managers make the mistake of assuming that because their time is valuable and because they spend so little time with individuals in their team, they attempt to put everything right on one visit. The aim of each visit should be to tackle one thing at a time.

How will this visit contribute to the short, medium, and long-term aims of the salesperson? If they can focus on the positive outcomes of the visit as contributing to a larger whole, the chances are they will also have a greater sense of purpose in improving their performance on each and every sale. In quality terms, this is the 'kaizen' principle of improving one step at a time. The performer is in a virtuous cycle of learning something new, practising it between coaching sessions and then addressing themselves to a higher target. The partnership between the coach and performer is a very important support to maintaining the performer's focus and motivation to stay on the path of continuous improvement.

A good personal aim for the salesperson and for the manager, as well as for the company, is to make the customer a lifetime customer. Ask the salesperson to think about the type of behaviour during an interview that would convince the customer that this is a worthy aim.

Is it Above or Below the Line?

Are you working with the salesperson to get them up to the line (the basic, benchmark, or minimum standards)? Or are they operating above the line, in which case you can coach them? If they are below the line, then that is training. You should not try to coach people in one area if there are elements of below-the-line activity that have not yet been mastered. If you try to coach people above the line whilst other basics remain unsatisfactory, it will undermine the coaching work. If it is training, then there is no negotiation of what to work on. If it is coaching, then the salesperson has a big influence on what to work on.

Observation

You should introduce yourself to the customer as the salesperson's manager. The customer will guess who you are anyway. Simply tell them that, as part of the quality controls of the company, you regularly go out on calls with the sales team. Say that you will not take part in the interview, but will sit quietly out of the way. It might seem awkward at first, but everyone concerned will soon forget you are there.

Stay out of sight of the customer if you can, but somewhere you can maintain eye contact with the salesperson. When they need moral support, they should be able to see you. Do not interrupt or interject unless it is absolutely necessary. If the salesperson misses a sales opportunity, provided you have trained them to always ask for the next appointment, you can always coach them to get the sale next time. If you interject and get the business, it will destroy the salesperson's confidence. If you interject and fail to get the business, it will destroy yours! If you can, develop some sort of code between you and the salesperson so that, if they need your help, they can ask for you to rescue them without actually saying it.

During the actual interview, your job is to concentrate on what is going on. You will have clarified your purpose and set out the parameters (the 'P' in POWER). Overall, you want to make certain that the rules are being followed. Specifically, you will already have agreed the objective with the salesperson (the 'O' in POWER) and you will be focusing on that. You cannot concentrate on more than one thing at a time either. Your task is to focus on what they are saying and doing, and the effect it is having on the customer.

Observe positive behaviours — for example, those behaviours that help the salesperson reach their objective. Positive behaviour could include:

- Actively seeking the prospect's opinions.
- Effective use of point-of-sale (POS) materials.
- Persuasive use of word pictures.
- Asking good probing questions.
- Listening well.

The list could be longer, shorter or totally different — it does not matter. For the salesperson, it represents the positive behaviours for the specific task. It is both motivating and instructive to provide feedback on those aspects of the performance that are producing positive results. You want to encourage the salesperson to repeat and build on those aspects that they are doing well.

Having focused in the first instance on the positive behaviours, then you must look at the behaviours which lead to negative outcomes. Use the Performance Wheels (**Figure 21**) to assist you in recording negative behaviours. Your list might include:

- Interrupted the customer.
- Poor eye contact with customer.
- Hesitant delivery during sales presentation.
- Poor use of POS material.
- Unable to explain relevant product features.
- Too much jargon.
- Did not explore customer needs adequately.

Discussion

After the sales interview comes the discussion, or at least that is the normal format. When talking with sales managers after a sales interview, salespeople are often waiting for them to say, "Well how do you think that went?" only for them to respond by saying, "Well, I think it was all right". The manager says a few words of wisdom, looks at their watch and disappears over the horizon muttering about meetings and the need to be elsewhere. Try and save your full discussion for the end of the day when you carry out your full feedback session. You cannot judge a performance on one interview. That is why you have to spend the whole day with a salesperson and, if possible, more than one day.

If you are the salesperson's line manager, it is impossible to be wholly objective or even to be seen to be objective. It is very important, therefore, to ask questions in such a way that there is no sense of blame or rebuke attached. For example, rather than asking "Why did you do that?", which may make the salesperson defensive rather than willing to open up, you could ask: "What factors did you consider when deciding what to do?".

Ask questions that seek feelings — not "How do you feel that went?" which always results in "Fine", but rather "What do you feel you did particularly well today?" and "What do you feel you could have done better?". The emphasis must be on specifics. Get the salesperson to self-evaluate first, before giving your observations.

Make the interaction conversational and keep it light-hearted. It is supposed to be helpful, not interrogative. If you have bad news to give, sugar the pill. Find something positive to say, even if it is only about the state of their shoes! Whatever you do, however, do not give comments, criticism or praise without giving examples. (For a detailed discussion on feedback, see also **Chapter 11, Review**.)

Examples of Good Questions to Ask at This Stage
For new starters:

- Let's now review what has actually happened since you started.
- Where are you compared to where we agreed you should be?
- What has been the main contributing factor to your performance?
- How could you have done better?
- What help have you received?
- Could you have done more?
- What obstacles have there been and how have you overcome them?

For those performing below the line:

- Tell me what you have been doing, and how you have been doing it.
- What have been the outcomes of this? (You may wish to deal with each separately.)
- So what you are saying is that this activity and the quality of this activity that you have been undertaking have produced this level and quality of results.
- What do you believe you now have to do in order to reach the benchmark level of output we need?

For those performing above the line:

- Tell me what you've been doing, and how you have been doing it.
- What have been the outcomes of this? (You may wish to deal with each separately.)
- What have been your major successes?
- What barriers have you encountered?
- How did you overcome them?
- Say you wanted to improve your performance output, what do you think you would have to do to accomplish that?

Clearly, your job with an over-the-line performer is to raise their expectations: "I have confidence in your ability and skill to perform even better than you are" or "I just know that you've got another 10 per cent in you — the question is, how can I help you achieve that?".

Consolidation

All the conversation and discussion in the world is no substitute for putting the theory into practice. The worst thing you can do is to say "OK, what I want you to do is to try this, and come back and tell me how you got on". People cannot alter their ways of doing things overnight, and certainly not after a few pearls of wisdom, no matter how right you might be. There is only one way to implement skills improvement: both you and the salesperson must commit yourselves to putting the theory into practice. The best way to do this is to practise sufficiently first until the skill becomes innate and then to observe the salesperson implementing the process in reality as soon as possible. This is empowerment (the 'E' in POWER), where the salesperson is empowered to implement a plan of action following the observation.

Get the salesperson to appraise themselves and, using the POWER© model, ask on a scale of one to 10 what the chances are of them implementing the plan. Then do it, agreeing a realistic review date (the 'R' in POWER).

Traps to Avoid

There are three traps that many sales managers fall into at this point:

- Telling people what their performance is.
- Asking them *why* their performance is at its current level.
- Delving even deeper to improve understanding.

I have covered the pitfalls of 'telling' earlier. It does not work and it does not produce ownership. You start out with the monkey and you end up with the monkey. It also tends to lead to a lot of background explanation and analysis, which is unhelpful because it shifts awareness away from reality. There are plenty of alternatives that are less threatening and more effective at raising awareness. On balance, it's better not to use 'why?' at all.

Another easy trap to fall into is delving deeper into the situation because you want to understand it, but it is not necessary for you as the coach to understand all the details. You are not asking the questions for your own sake. As a coach, your aim is to raise their awareness and to enable them to focus on appropriate areas so that they can identify their own problems and find their own solutions.

At the end of this stage, it is worth checking whether the original goal is still valid, because many people find they wish to modify it in the light of reality.

A COACHING VISIT WITHOUT OBSERVATION

From time to time, you will meet up with the salesperson, and may conduct a coaching session without observation of the salesperson in front of a customer. This might include basic training (e.g., role-play), setting of short, medium and long-term objectives and performance reviews. However, I have very strong views about non-observation visits, in that the measure of all of the work that you undertake with a salesperson only ever can be assessed by observing the salesperson interacting with a customer. Although I believe that role play is real in that you use real words and body language, the game has to be played on the pitch to determine whether it is effective or not. What I suggest is that, at the very least, every other meeting with the salesperson should be an observation.

THE ROAD TO CHAMPIONSHIP PERFORMANCE

As I said earlier, the objectives and standards salespeople set themselves within a coaching programme are often higher than that which the company or the sales manager demands or expects. Your task now is to see what the current performance is so that you can look at the steps the performer needs to undertake to reach the desired performance.

In addition, it is at this point that you establish the rules with regard to personal responsibility. You need to make it quite clear that the actions, behaviours, and attitudes employed by the salesperson have an effect. Inputs equal outputs. The salesperson is solely responsible for the results they achieve, good, bad or indifferent. Yet my experience shows that most sales managers focus their attention on bad performance and, in the frustration experienced, end up telling people to get their finger out — or see more people, the activity trap described earlier. In fact, the more time you spend with top performers, the greater the potential return you will achieve. Improving the results of someone producing 50,000 units per year by five per cent will provide you with a greater payback than improving the results of someone producing 20,000 units by 10 per cent.

Begin this process by asking the performer to assess their own performance through a series of questions.

SETTING UP THE DISCUSSION

If you are about to hold a first coaching session with someone and your purpose is to help them improve their performance, you should make it clear to them that they need to bring an analysis of their performance to the coaching session with them. You also need to prepare, but the aim of them doing so is to apply some rules to the coaching sessions you intend to undertake. All too often, managers turn up with reams of analysis which the salesperson has not seen before and, as a consequence, the salesperson becomes overwhelmed.

Insisting that salespeople come to coaching sessions prepared should be part of the rules of basic training. They provide the tools with which to analyse performance and to set goals for improvement. By making the salesperson turn up with their own data and analysis, you put the responsibility onto them for their performance as well as teaching them that they should be keeping track personally of their performance.

SOME QUESTIONS TO ASK

What have you done about it so far? Has the salesperson really done anything about progressing toward their goal, other than talk about it? People are talented at setting themselves fantastic goals which, if implemented, would change their lives forever. The landscape is littered with goals that never got off the drawing board because nobody asked the question: "What have you done about it so far?". Merely asking the question can be a spur to action. The problem is that, as individuals, we never ask ourselves this question. That is why the role of the coach is important.

We might talk to ourselves, but if the questions we ask ourselves start becoming tricky, we pretend we did not hear them, or change the question. Even if we ask ourselves: "What have I done about it so far?", we tend to say: "Actually, quite a bit", or "Well, I have not had a lot of time", or "What was the question?".

Acting as coach, the sales manager helps to examine specific actions — not appraising, just asking. The salesperson will know how to judge the response. Faced with someone who asks us the right questions, we do not need any judgement; we can do that for ourselves. When the salesperson says: "I suppose you think ..." or "You are probably saying ...", the coach should reply "At this stage, I have no opinion. What you think is more important than my opinion. What do you think?".

What was the result? By this stage, the salesperson will have opened the floodgates of self-awareness. Talking about our goals, our attempts at starting the journey and the reality of our experiences is very therapeutic. The focus on reality by the salesperson, merely verbalising what they already know internally — that the last course of action did not bring the desired results or failed to deliver all of the results — is enough. You should encourage the salesperson to use descriptive language, such as "I was 10 per cent below my sales conversion target", rather than the general "I was bad at converting prospects into sales".

You are likely to encounter a range of excuses at this stage, as the performer seeks to pin the blame on someone or something else. Our inner self is very good at coming up with excuses: "I did my best ...", "It nearly worked out ...", "I did not get the support ...", "The bottom dropped out of the market ..." and so on. The list can be as long as individuals are prepared to talk to themselves. Regardless of the depth of the internal conversation, the fact still remains that it is seldom verbalised. Talking out aloud to yourself can land you in serious trouble, especially if you adopt the full coaching practice and answer back! We simply do not ask ourselves the right questions. We know what they should be; it just seems that we are unable to vocalise them.

The question facilitates the performer to accept responsibility for the result. There is seldom a need for the coach to say: "And who is responsible for that result?". In fact, the danger of doing so is that the performer then can think of someone else who in his or her opinion might be responsible for the failure. It is best for the coach to say nothing. A simple shrug will do. The coach needs to be able to display the correct body language at the appropriate time.

What have the obstacles been? Examining the obstacles at this stage has two effects. One is that it could save you some considerable time listening to how much other people, events, and the world at large are to blame, and the second is that the performer will normally have decided that they themselves are the biggest obstacle.

How did you set about overcoming them? This reinforces whose responsibility it is to move the process forward. Had the salesperson taken suitable action before, the session might not be necessary at all. But then, with hindsight, we could all have done it differently.

What would you now do differently? Each question builds on the one before. Nowhere in any of this does the coach instruct. The coach may have some tremendous ideas and may have seen it all before, but it is what the performer comes up with that is relevant, and it is what the salesperson identifies as being the solution that will work.

There is much greater ownership when the performer sets out what they would do differently.

In the next chapter, I look at how you can work with the salesperson to capitalise on the self-awareness you have engendered and work on habits that are inhibiting a peak performance. I call the next phase 'Empowerment'.

CHAPTER 10

EMPOWERMENT

Champions are not made in gyms. Champions are made
from something they have deep inside them — a desire, a
dream, a vision. They have to have last-minute stamina,
they have to be a little faster, they have to have the skill
and the will. But the will must be stronger than the skill.

Muhammad Ali

Empowerment, like many of the fad expressions of the last few years,
has suffered from a bad press. Yet empowerment is more than simply
passing the baton onto someone else. It is also about creating an
environment in which someone wants to pick up the baton in the first
place.

I have spent some time talking about the coach's vision, but what
of the salesperson's vision? What does he or she want to achieve? Do
they have the will to succeed (as highlighted in the Ali quote)? As
covered in **Chapter 8, Objectives and Options**, will the execution of a
planned course of action lead towards the achievement of the
individual's goals? Unless there is some connection between vision,
objective, and empowerment, then the chances are that the effort
needed to succeed will be less than is required.

In addition, it can happen that, on the journey towards a goal,
either you or the salesperson takes a new route. There is nothing
wrong with changing course, provided that the journey is always
forward. The individual might believe that it is all right to regroup
and to take stock before moving forward. You might even hear
people say that sometimes you have to take one step back to go two
steps forward. This may be true, but who pays the piper whilst he is
learning the new tune? In the commercial world, it is all too easy for

people to believe that resources are easily available to pay for learning. Indeed, many organisations actively promote themselves as a learning organisation without realising the true cost of such a generous offer. Whilst I have nothing against people learning — I believe strongly in the maxim 'to stop learning is to stop living' — these questions need to be asked: "Who is paying for this? And what is it adding to the bottom line?". A balance needs to be struck between the organisation's needs and those of the individual.

By asking probing questions to help raise self-awareness and by observing the salesperson in action, this should have enabled you to analyse the salesperson's performance in terms of positive and negative behaviours. The next stage is to see what can be done to improve those aspects of the performance that are stopping the individual from reaching their goals. You are now at the fourth stage of the POWER© coaching model, where you need the salesperson to take responsibility for making things happen, for making improvements, and for contracting with you to work on an action plan.

I talk a lot about the value of practice in this chapter. The adage 'practice makes perfect' is true. The salesperson must draw up an action plan that will empower them through practice to deliver an enhanced sales performance, to reach that higher goal that is beyond their current performance standard – a 'championship performance'.

EMPOWERING

Empowerment means placing the responsibility for the performance on the individual. At the moment of execution of the coaching plan by the individual, it is the salesperson who is responsible.

For empowerment to work, the manager must have absolute trust in the individual's capacity to succeed. The salesperson, in turn, must have trust in the manager that mistakes will be tolerated. Too many people operate on the basis of not making mistakes, and yet without mistakes and learning from them, people will never experience success. Empowering people means allowing them to find their way. It is the cornerstone of coaching. It shows an ultimate belief in the ability of the salesperson to achieve. Empowering people means treating them as adults who are capable of making decisions for themselves, especially the routine decisions that clog up the normal day of a manager.

By creating an empowering environment, work will take on a new meaning for many. People want to be involved. If it appears to you that the contrary exists in your company, then it probably has more to do with the way in which people are treated, or have been treated in the past. And just because you tried it once and it did not work, do not assume that it will not work in the future. Remember, if you have operated in a certain way for a number of years, then it is unreasonable to expect people to change just because you change the way you treat them for a fortnight.

FORCED CHANGE

The theory of empowering people is all right so far as it goes. We need to understand that we are sometimes taking people outside of their comfort zones, and they will resist this process. This is especially so in selling, where the improvements you are seeking almost always involve implementation in front of a customer. Everything can be perfect in the training room and on the practice pitch, but the ultimate measure is what happens in front of the customer. Self-development can be an uncomfortable process, especially when we try to change the habits of a lifetime. Experience can be extremely valuable, but it can also act as a major barrier to learning and to trying new things.

Try folding your arms in the opposite way to how you normally do it. How do you feel? It is an uncomfortable feeling. With any forced change, we must go through an uncomfortable learning process. I have identified five stages of this process:

- Denial.
- Anger.
- Bargaining.
- Depression.
- Acceptance.

It is only when we reach the acceptance stage that we really start to learn and develop as people. If that stage is not reached, we continue to live in the past and repeat our former habits and behaviours. In a coaching relationship, you are not seeking to push change on the individual. The natural reaction to push energy is resistance. When change is forced on people, they have to pass through many stages before reaching grudging acceptance. In such circumstances, you will not achieve anything higher than a mediocre performance. You can only unlock the salesperson's true potential when the energy is coming from within.

One of the key tasks of a coach is to encourage and support the salesperson through the setbacks and impediments that will stand in their way. The salesperson may have to go through pain, self-doubt and enormous effort to reach medium- and long-range goals. If you are dealing with a top performer, you have the additional challenge of encouraging them to reach even higher goals. But peak performers are driven to improve their personal bests, even when they are better than those competing with them.

Sometimes you hear athletes talking about the 'perfect race'. They feel relaxed, happy and totally focused on winning. They are not worried about their running technique or race strategy — that has all been worked out a long time ago through the hundreds of practice sessions preparing for the big race. They have reached a level of unconscious competence in their sport: they no longer have to think about how to run; their minds are freed up so they can focus on winning. In any other physical skill, such as playing an instrument or acting in a play, the performers are not thinking about the skill needed to put in a good performance. These skills have become unconscious competencies. Their minds are focused on creating a great performance. They are thinking at a higher level.

The acquisition of knowledge and skills is a lifelong commitment. In recent years, the rate of change has become so fast that products are often obsolete within a year, and processes change almost as quickly. If our organisation is not moving at a quicker pace than the pace of our industry as a whole, then effectively we are going backwards. As managers and as team players, all of us must continue to gain expertise but avoid thinking of ourselves as experts.

However, change remains a difficult element to cope with for everyone. Yet by forcing the salesperson to practise new skills, we increase the confidence that comes from mastering a new skill and, in the process, we can reduce the resistance to change so normal in all of us. We need to consciously practise those skills we think we have mastered. Golfers practise, footballers train, musicians rehearse. Learning and practice never end, so regardless of whether you are coaching a peak performer or a salesperson who is facing certain basic difficulties, the rule is still the same: practise, practise, practise.

I particularly remember a classic example of forced change from my own experience. I was working in the insurance division of a large financial institution. The building my department was in was to be renovated, and some 600 people had to be relocated to other offices, five miles away, for a period of at least six months. Although faced with immediate change, and not being too keen about the prospect and the disruption, the actual move was quickly resolved for most staff. It is possible to go through all the stages of change very quickly – for example:

- I cannot believe they want us to move out. (Denial)
- It's a disgrace. How am I supposed to work under these conditions? (Anger)
- What about if we left it until we have finished this project? (Bargaining)
- It's no good, the project will suffer, and it's a disaster. (Withdrawal)
- OK, I cannot do anything about it, let's get on with it. (Acceptance)

For me, however, it was a different story. The first thing that happened to me was that I was separated from my colleagues, and put into an area in another part of the building with other managers, in what was euphemistically called a 'pig-pen' – a small area with a desk, a chair, a cupboard and three dividing screens. It was possible, although it required some athleticism, to touch all the boundaries of the space without moving from my desk. My own experience of the five stages began immediately.

Denial: I cannot believe this. This has to be a mistake. I telephoned the person responsible for allocating space. "John, I've got a problem here. I've been put in an area where I shouldn't be." I explained the situation. It was right. This was where I had to be. I sat down. "No, this cannot be right." I telephoned someone else. It was right. "No, this cannot be right, it does not make sense." Much of the first day was spent checking it out. Day two of the move dawned. The next stage locked in.

Anger: "I'm not having this." I went to the area where my staff were. For the rest of the day, they ran for cover as I stomped around. "This is ridiculous. I cannot work in these conditions. Who do they think they are? This place is a mess. Get it cleaned up. How much space have you got? You do not need all this space. Where am I going to put my books? What have you done about fixing the computer line?" The point about anger is that, while releasing frustration in some way, it is a fruitless activity with only negative consequences. For a short while, it made me feel better, but it hardly enhanced staff relations. Day three dawned and stage three arrived as if by clockwork.

Bargaining: I walked around the building, and on the next floor up I found an empty office and another next to it with only stationery in it. "John, there is an empty office on the next floor up, can I have that? Oh, I see. Well, the one next door only has stationery in it. If I got it moved, could I use that as an office?" I was told that it would be needed in two months by another department. "Well, that's OK, I'll move again later." The idea was not well received. I approached my own boss. "Peter, I need your help." It did not work. I went back to my secretary. "Mary, what about if we moved you and Julie into that space, and I moved into this one? Alan, if you got rid of that equipment, and turned your desk around, we could have a bit of space here. You know this office for three of you is full of cupboards. If we put them into storage, I could have this office." Nothing worked.

There is no guarantee that progress through these changes is linear. You can go backwards – and I did. "This is just stupid [back to anger]. There must have been a mistake [denial]." You can also go briefly forward, and I did. It turns out there was a mistake. I was missed off the original plans. Worse still, I was to blame (withdrawal). "I do not believe it (denial). Well, somebody better get his or her finger out (anger). As I was missed off the original plans, and wasn't supposed to be here anyway, obviously I need to be where I was supposed to be (bargaining)." Nothing worked. Day four arrived.

Withdrawal: I sat in my space. All around me was noise. As I peered over the screen behind me, I could see other people happily working away. "I cannot work here. This is awful. This is impossible. It's dreadful. My work will suffer. The project might as well be cancelled. Why me?" Mary came in to see me. I went up and down the stages again. "Look at this place – it's a mad house (anger). I cannot believe this is happening (denial and withdrawal). What about if we moved the desk the other way around (bargaining)?" It was moved. It was not any better. "It's worse (withdrawal). I want to know who missed me off the plans (anger)." It was my boss. "I knew it. It's outrageous (anger). But nobody's going to change his or her mind – it's hopeless (withdrawal)." Friday – day five.

Acceptance: "This is pointless. I cannot do anything about it. It's a case of like it or lump it, but I've got a job to do." I worked late for a month making up the wasted time but I finished the project to schedule. When we moved back to the original building six months later, my office had disappeared. "I do not believe it!"

CHECK IT OUT

Your first job following any training intervention is to check whether someone, in the face of forced change, has moved forward to acceptance or not. It is pointless trying to implement a coaching plan when the salesperson has not rationalised in their own mind that they want to do it in the first place. You cannot coach people who have not accepted their need for change. If the salesperson does not know the reason for behavioural change, it is your responsibility to identify the reason or reasons for change and to help them to understand why it is necessary.

And what about you? My experience tells me that moving from sales management to sales coaching is not as straightforward as it may seem. For a start, sales coaching involves a lot of doing, and behavioural change. Just because we are managers does not mean that we accept the need to change any more readily than salespeople. Have you ever been through the five stages of forced change? What happened? How did you feel?

When you know the stages, it becomes easier to handle the process. The sooner each of us gets to acceptance the better. That does not mean, however, that for most us just accepting the situation works. Most of us have to go through the process. Realising what the process is helps us both to help ourselves and also to recognise what is happening to others.

EMPOWERING QUESTIONS

When you are at the empowerment stage and your salesperson is about to draw up their action plan for future focus, there are many questions that the coach can ask.

So what do you have to do about it now? At this point, the performer could say: "I suppose what you are telling me is ..." or something similar. Many salespeople have a lifetime of being told what to do behind them and, even at this stage in the process, they may seek to put the responsibility for potential failure onto the coach. The coach needs to make the salesperson absolutely aware of whose responsibility it now is to move forward. For example, "I'm not telling you anything at this stage. Whatever you do is up to you. You are responsible for your performance".

What is it you want to do now? Having gained that commitment, it is important to reinforce it: "Is that what you want to do? How much trust do you have in your ability to do it?".

At this juncture, it becomes important to measure the performer's level of commitment. Is the performer doing it because they really want to, or is it some external influence, such as the coach, that is making them do it? Unless the salesperson is convinced both that they have the ability and that success is possible, it is likely that they will fail. A strong supplementary question now is: "On a scale of one to 10, what is the likelihood of you succeeding or of carrying out this task?". If the salesperson identifies the likelihood of success as being at seven or below, then the chances are that they will not succeed, and the process should begin again. The coach may also decide that further investment of their time is now questionable. Remember, coaching is not counselling. The coach has aims and, in the case of the coach being a manager, they may also have urgent organisational goals to achieve. It is quite in order for the coach, having heard a commitment of less than seven, to say: "I now have a problem in investing more of my time in something which you feel has a less than certain chance of success".

The discussion following this statement can be enlightening. At this stage, the coach and salesperson can revisit the goal, redefine the deadline, or examine why the salesperson does not appear totally committed. It could be the wrong goal, which is why the questions are powerful. Many people invest energy in ill-defined goals, which, because they have not been examined in detail, often fail to be realised.

What immediate support do you need? The contract is a joint one. The salesperson needs to feel that there is support, and the coach needs to offer it. The achievement of the goal also may require additional resources, such as equipment, people support or further training. This is that last chance to get it right before going for the goal.

Can you see any personal barriers that might hold you back? It is useful at this stage to help the salesperson to consider the types of personal issues that might cause them to be deflected from their goal. You may find that the salesperson lacks confidence in certain situations. Through visualising the performance of the goal and talking through the issues that can upset the person's concentration or focus, the salesperson can address the problems in advance in an environment where they feel safe.

Are there any other issues that could impede your performance? There may be certain market or organisational changes that the performer feels will reduce his or her chance of success. It is important to anticipate and deal with these issues before the coaching session ends, as these external barriers to performance could become the excuses for non-completion. In answering this question, the salesperson is obliged to think of contingency plans in advance.

Do it! The coach empowers the individual to achieve the goal. The instruction is directive. Throughout the whole process, the coach has avoided telling the salesperson what to do, precisely because the time to tell is now and it therefore has maximum impact. That is not to say that during the rest of the process the coach may not offer advice, but only after asking for permission.

'Do it' should be the first and only time in the initial stages that the coach tells the salesperson what to do, and yet the coach is not really telling the salesperson what to do, but rather merely telling the salesperson to do what the salesperson has identified as the correct course of action.

In this phase, we should be discussing specifically the salesperson's commitment to practise a new skill, checking with the salesperson when they will start, the frequency with which they will be able to practise the skill and so on. Get the salesperson to discuss specific dates, clients, etc.

When setting out their action plan, it is vital that the salesperson does not bite off more than they can chew. In other words, the action plan should have a maximum of three points for improvement. An improvement in performance typically stems from a focus on one step at a time — remember, we are trying to lift the bar just one little notch at a time.

CHAPTER 11

REVIEW

The greatest accomplishment is not in never failing, but
in rising again after you fall. *Vince Lombardi*

One of the most challenging aspects of achieving peak performance is
the requirement to change deeply-embedded habits. Training or pep
talks on their own cannot help you to change behaviour. The review
of a performance is a very powerful tool to help embed behavioural
change. You can review immediately after a course of action has been
agreed. You can ask the performer to role-play a particular
interaction that requires improvement. You can also review a
performance after the salesperson has been given a period of time to
practise a new task. The review uses the coaching tools of
questioning, observation, role-play and feedback. In this chapter, I
examine what the 'R' means in the POWER© model. Specifically, I will
focus on how you as coach can keep the performer on track, even if
they go slightly off course every now and then!

A review is used at two stages in the coaching process:
immediately after a new course of action has been followed and at
the commencement of a session within a whole coaching programme.

IMMEDIATE REVIEW

Coaching only works if, following agreement on a course of action,
the coach then observes the salesperson carrying out the task
immediately. By immediately offering to observe, the coach again
tests the commitment of the salesperson. This also shows the
commitment of the coach to help the salesperson succeed.

PROGRESS REVIEW

A coaching partnership takes place over time, and that is its special value. You review performance over time and raise the performance bar a little at each session, but you also need to observe what has happened and check back on your agreed action plan from the previous coaching session.

Did the salesperson do what they said they would do? This discussion cannot take place without the coach having been there to observe what happened. Getting feedback from a salesperson about what they did and what happened without first-hand knowledge is a pointless and fruitless exchange. The coach observes and compares against what was agreed: "What were you trying to do? What did you do? What did you feel? Where did you feel it? What would you do differently?".

The process is the same as that which went before. The added advantage is that now both coach and salesperson have additional data to hand — experience of the event. It can prove invaluable.

THE CHAMPION'S JOURNAL

If it is not written down, it did not happen. Unless you write something down at the time and refer to it in the future, you and the salesperson must rely on memory. It is virtually a certainty that your recollection of events will be different from that of the performer's. *The Champion's Journal* (see **Appendix 1**) is the ideal way to record plans and achievements and can be used to track performance over a series of coaching sessions. It is vital that, as a coach, you keep a log to record and monitor the action plan. In turn, the salesperson must also keep a copy of their agreed action plan.

In addition, a *Champion's Journal* is a personal log for training and development that the salesperson undertakes to keep for the duration of the coaching programme. This log allows the salesperson to record activities or achievements that they are proud of or that are important milestones to reaching a personal goal or ambition.

While it is the salesperson's choice to use the log or not, it is worth remembering that they will find it hard to stay on track if they are not aiming towards goals that are clearly stated. Equally, if they do not log their successes, the development needs they have, and the positive changes that will result, how can they be certain they have actually achieved them? Sometimes, it can be comforting to be able to remind ourselves of our ability to achieve and our willingness to learn through looking back at the written word. This exercise also can be motivational for the salesperson to continue on the onward path of achievement.

CHANGING BEHAVIOUR

While the salesperson may have understood and agreed to improve specific skills or behaviour, they are likely to have found the reality of trying to change behaviour on the job much more difficult than they thought. In the review session, you may need to discuss the special challenges of changing behaviour. You also may encounter some resistance from salespeople who think you are trying to change their personality!

Many people confuse personality with behaviour, so it is important to emphasise that you are not trying to change the salesperson's personality. A person's personality is unique and includes characteristics such as temperament, emotional and mental traits and patterns of behaviour. In a coaching relationship, we are concerned only with the salesperson's observable behaviour on the job, and that behaviour can be changed, though it takes a lot of time and effort.

You may find that the salesperson does not accept that behavioural change is possible, but you can illustrate how much the salesperson has changed by asking questions about how they approached the job when they first started working compared to their current approach. While we learn a lot about how to interact with people from a very early age, we also learn much of our behaviour on the job. Depending on the type of organisation, the leadership style and the people who we learn from at work, we can grow or improve — or regress and worsen. We are changing and adapting all the time. The idea that we are stuck in some sort of behavioural groove just does not stack up.

Remembering that selling is a physical skill, like sports or the performing arts. Behavioural change in all these activities comes about through experimentation and practice. The salesperson also typically finds that they reduce performance while they are experimenting and practising. It may take weeks or even months. We need to practise a new behaviour until it becomes an unconscious competence (see **Chapter 1**).

ROLE-PLAYS

We have discussed the importance of practice a good deal. It is not unusual, however, for salespeople to find the notion of practising before they go out in front of a 'live audience' (their customers) fussy, unnecessary and even insulting to their intelligence. My own research has shown that salespeople always will choose training on product knowledge when asked to identify training needs, while role-play consistently is at the bottom of the list. Most salespeople, except the good ones, will try to avoid any environment in which they have to sell or practise their selling skills.

The letters ROLE could well stand for 'Rehearsal of Live Events', because role-play sessions are meant to prepare people for situations that might happen. The role-plays you use should be about situations that have happened or are likely to happen in the future. To prepare for this, you should build up a series of case studies based on the combined experience of the sales force. Take time to develop some scripts and scenarios that will produce the ideal learning point you are seeking to achieve.

When faced with a salesperson who is reluctant to participate in role-plays, ask them: "If you do not believe in the need to practise through role-play, then are you saying that you'll practise live in a customer meeting?". The penny should drop! Professionals in sport or the performing arts must practise before performing live.

Poor performance through lack of rehearsal time equals poor sales.

BE POSITIVE

When reviewing team or individual performances, the sales coach should remember the lessons highlighted earlier in the Pygmalion effect (**Chapter 5**). In a coaching role, it is imperative that you affirm individuals' efforts to enhance their own performance.

The process starts with the coach, in that how you feel about yourself will impact on how others see or feel about you. If you feel optimistic and believe that your sales team can deliver the required results, then your positive style will affect your people and their self-belief. The reverse is also true. In case you think that your mood or outlook is outside your own control, remember that you, and you alone, have the power to choose your own outlook and response in any situation. Victor Frankl put it succinctly:

> The last of the human freedoms (is) to choose one's attitude in any given set of circumstances, to choose one's own way.[27]

No sales team, nor indeed any team, will perform to its true potential unless people in the team feel valued. The coach is key, as you can provide the necessary support structure for increased individual productivity. This means, for example, that the sales manager should always be on the lookout for positive behaviours or results. Never allow a sales interview in which you have observed the salesperson in action go by without finding something positive to say — even where a sale did not result.

The coach's attitude and the language used are very important when giving feedback. When you have positive things to say to the performer, use words like 'great', 'excellent', 'top class', or 'terrific' when commenting on their fine performance. Do not wait for a big sale to offer praise. Instead, recognise the small steps of achievement and, in this way, plant the seeds of success for a bigger harvest. Your team will respond more positively to your expressions of enthusiasm and optimism. This becomes a reinforcer and they are much more likely to repeat their successful sales behaviours. In this way, it can

---

[27] Victor Frankl, *Man's Search for Meaning*, First Washington Square Press, 1985.

become a cycle of success. Over time, watch the body language of your sales team change for the better:

> Their expressions, postures and attitudes change when you enter the room. Their backs will straighten, the corners of their mouths will turn up, and they will unconsciously reflect your positive spirit, in spite of themselves. But here's the good news: managers who have tested upbeat language in the workplace report that after a while just entering the office or building will produce positive staff response.[28]

However, offer praise only when it is warranted. Over-praising when there is no evidence of achievement or effort will fool no-one. Indeed, it can do more harm than good, in that it will tend to negate genuinely positive output.

BE HONEST

When coaching Wexford, the All Ireland Hurling champions of 1996, to success, coach Liam Griffin stated that their success was built on the principles of trust and honesty.[29] This need for honesty between coach and players is a common feature among other successful sports teams and in the performing arts, and it holds true for the sales coach. When reviewing someone's performance after their own self-analysis, be direct, open and honest with them. Focus on what you actually observed. Highlight with the salesperson where you have points of agreement with their own analysis but also do not be afraid to highlight areas where you disagree. Cite specific examples in your discussion.

You owe it to them and to yourself to be honest. Tell them the truth, even when at times it will hurt. If you take the easy way out and fudge feedback in a review with your salespeople, it will come back to haunt you. How can people progress unless they know how they are currently performing?

---

[28] William Hendricks (ed.), *Coaching, Mentoring and Managing*, Career Press, 1996.

[29] *Coaching Champions: The Wexford Team Story*, a training video made by First Active plc Training & Development, 1996.

FEEDBACK

Feedback is sometimes called the 'breakfast of champions'. Providing feedback is an essential part of coaching.

There are two main reasons for giving feedback:

- To reward people when they are doing well, known as motivational feedback.

- To help and encourage performers to improve, termed developmental feedback.

How much, how often and how you do it is critical. Too much, too often and too critical can result in a de-motivated salesperson who only learns how to comply, not to excel. Your job as a coach is to give feedback in such a way that the salesperson is encouraged to move on. That does not mean ignoring areas that require improvement, but you have to understand that none of us likes negative feedback.

Focus on Behaviour, Not Attitude

Never mention attitude (e.g., "You do not seem to have the right attitude for the job"). Attitude is a consequence of behaviour. You could be right that their attitude is wrong, yet you will never change it by talking about it. In the same way that talking about a failure to meet targets will not result in target achievement, talking about a bad attitude will not result in achieving positive behaviour.

Failure to achieve target is a consequence of actions taken by the salesperson. The way you improve achievement of target is to examine the actions taken by the salesperson. The way to improve attitude is to examine the behaviours that cause the attitude. You can retrain behaviours, but you cannot retrain attitude. Behaviours can be observed; attitudes can only be felt.

How to Deliver High-Impact Feedback

Throughout the whole coaching relationship, you are providing feedback or acting as a mirror to the salesperson so that they can 'see' themselves more clearly. Feedback is essential to development. For feedback to be effective, it must be given in a safe, collaborative climate that is non-threatening. If you adopt a cross-examining style, the salesperson will become defensive.

The following tips can be applied in many coaching and non-coaching situations:

- **Time and place:** Feedback should take place as quickly as possible after the event in order to achieve maximum impact. Always conduct feedback sessions in private and ensure that there are no interruptions, such as phone calls. If either the coach or salesperson is under stress, postpone the feedback session.

- **Encourage the performer to do the talking:** Use a questioning approach so that you give the salesperson the opportunity to discover their own learning, as well as letting them know that you value their opinion.

- **Establish trust:** Your sales team should believe that you will support them in their performance efforts and that your role is to help them to deliver on the sales goals. In the feedback session, adopt a partnership relationship. If you can show that you are on the same side as the salesperson – there to help and support, not admonish and undermine – then you will help to build up trust and achieve better results. Where a performance problem exists, for example, do not say "You've got a problem", instead say "We've got a problem". This will help the salesperson to open up in the review more because you have adopted a joint 'we are in this together' approach. The responsibility for performance still rests with the salesperson.

- **Diagnose before you prescribe:** Try to really understand the salesperson's barriers and motivations. Listen closely to what they say and how they say it, then make sure they feel understood and accepted. You do not have to approve, and often you will not. You just need to demonstrate that you understand.

- **Do not hog the controls:** As the line manager, you will probably be perceived as having all the power. Share the control by allowing the salesperson to shape some of the feedback process, e.g., the focus of the feedback session. Remember that the salesperson's perception of what is important is more significant than your own observations.

- **Treat feedback as information, not as a value judgment:** Present feedback in neutral terms rather than labelling the behaviour or the person. Reward achievement by catching the salesperson doing things right.
- **Relate to performance objectives and expectations and keep the focus on behaviour, not personality or attitude:** For example: "I felt that you did not give your full attention to the sales enquiry" is far more beneficial than a sweeping statement such as "You are careless when dealing with sales enquiries".
- **Guide the feedback session:** Towards action points, a deadline and a commitment to review.
- **Concentrate on a maximum of three action points:** Reach agreement on benefits and consequences of the salesperson delivering on their action plan.
- **Start and finish on a positive note:** Highlight the benefits for the performer in undertaking the agreed action plan between coaching sessions.

Avoid the following feedback traps:
- Making suggestions without asking, e.g., "If I were you, what I would do is ...".
- Stating opinions, not facts.
- Trying to improve more than one thing at a time.
- Giving only bad news — emphasise the positive.
- Telling.
- Making sweeping statements and generalisations.
- Comparing performance to that of other people.
- Not giving examples.
- Not giving regular feedback.
- Not giving feedback soon after the observed behaviour.

Check that feedback has been received:
- Are they smiling?

- Are they making eye contact?
- Do they look puzzled or angry?
- Do they want to discuss the next steps?
- Are they looking withdrawn or concerned?
- Are they making notes and recording actions?
- Can they summarise the key points?

A FIVE-STEP FEEDBACK FORMAT

1. **Ask what worked:** By finding out what the salesperson thinks first using a questioning approach, you allow them the opportunity to discover for themselves what was positive in the performance. By beginning with a 'What worked?' question, you are showing that you value the positive aspects of the performance. This approach also will help the salesperson and coach to tune in on the same wavelength and to build rapport.

2. **Ask what did not work:** Having asked what worked, it is now easier to manage defensiveness about what did not work. By keeping the conversation focused on the process, you help the salesperson to reduce self-doubt and fear of criticism. The focus is on improvement, not blame. Concentrate on specifics and look for examples of observed behaviour.

3. **Ask what they might do differently next time:** This question opens the way for the salesperson to look at actionable points that require improvement. Keep the salesperson focused on changing just one to three parts of the performance. If you go for more, then the salesperson may become overwhelmed.

4. **Offer to give your own observations:** "Would you like any further suggestions from me?". By not jumping in at the beginning with your observations, you have allowed your relationship to become a partnership. This question will probably be met by "Yes", because the salesperson is keen to learn what you might be able to add to *their* thinking. Address those points that have been analysed by the salesperson. If you have further points written down, try to keep them for another session. Remember, if there are

several areas of improvement, you do not eat the elephant in one sitting.

5. **Work out an agreement:** Ask the salesperson to propose a solution; if necessary, you then propose your own. Agree upon an explicit action plan. Check understanding and commitment. Ask them to summarise their action points. Ensure both of you write these points down in your respective logs, which essentially is a record of the coaching session. Agree your next review date and time.

TYPES OF FEEDBACK

There are four types of feedback:

- Silence.
- Criticism (negative).
- Advice.
- Reinforcement (positive).

Silence:

- Can decrease confidence.
- Reduces performance in the long term.
- Gives people no benchmark.
- Creates problems when performance is low and reviews are held.
- Can make people feel insecure.

Criticism (negative):

- Produces excuses.
- Rarely gets at the root cause of low performance.
- Causes resentment (you never catch me doing things right).
- Decreases confidence and self-esteem.
- Leads to avoidance of meetings and discussions.

Advice:

- Can sometimes be ignored, or a poor result following an advisory session can be blamed on you.
- If delivered sensitively, can improve confidence.
- Can improve the relationship.
- Can increase performance.
- In all cases, should be accompanied by examples and observations.

Reinforcement (positive):

- Positive reinforcement is the best form of feedback.
- Increases confidence.
- Increases performance.
- Increases motivation.
- Encourages people to try new tasks and take risks.
- Reinforces positive behaviour, which should result in repetition of the positive action.

THE FEEDBACK LOOP

The review process may show that some of your original goals and objectives need to be revised or you even may wish to reconsider the whole value of the coaching process if you are encountering non-co-operation over a period of time. The review process therefore should feed back into the earlier phases of the coaching process, so that the process adapts to the individual needs and achievements of the salesperson.

The review makes the process never-ending, which is what you want — remember, no one is so good they cannot get better. Each new coaching session begins with the purpose and parameters. After the first coaching session, each subsequent purpose and parameters section in the coaching session should begin with a review of the last meeting.

WRITE EVERYTHING DOWN

There is a saying used in Compliance departments which says "If it is not written down, it did not happen". What I am not advocating is that you have to write down short novels of coaching interventions with your sales team, but you do need to keep a record of each intervention. This need be no more than a few lines recorded in the format of the POWER© coaching model, which I have included as **Appendix 2**. A copy of the form should be given to the salesperson soon after the coaching session, and you keep a copy on file.

The next time you meet with the salesperson again (which should not be too long afterwards), you can produce the form in order to review what happened last time, and to help focus you on the coaching session in hand.

CHAPTER 12

TAKING A REALITY CHECK

*It's a funny thing about life but, if you refuse to accept
anything but the very best, you will very often get it.*
W. Somerset Maugham

ORGANISATIONAL CULTURE

Sales coaching as a sales management function is a relatively recent activity. As such, it has emerged as a management technique rather than a function or job description. Look at any organisational chart and whilst 'sales manager' may appear as a job title, 'sales coach' probably will not. Yet in other professions such as sports, the title 'coach' is not only well-known but it is also well-respected. That is not to say that sales coaching as a job function is not respected – perhaps it may just be misunderstood.

Then there is the issue of culture. I would argue that, for sales coaching to be effective, the organisation needs to adopt a sales coaching culture, but exactly what does that mean? If the purpose of sales coaching is to improve the performance of the salesperson, it needs to be borne in mind that there are many influences on the performance of an individual salesperson (**Figure 22**).

The way in which salespeople carry out their job relies on their existing level of knowledge and skills and, more importantly, on how they choose to use that knowledge and skill – their attitude. It could be said that their attitude towards the job is greatly influenced by the role that the boss has and the way he/she has allowed the salesperson to do the job, and the habits the salesperson has acquired over a period. The way in which the manager operates and the manner in which he/she behaves towards the salesperson also will have been influenced by the culture of the organisation, which in turn is influenced by the external environment. Therefore, if the organisation does not have a sales coaching culture, simply sending sales managers on a sales coaching course or changing their job titles to 'sales coach' will not change anything if the organisation itself is of a different culture. Changing organisational culture is no easy thing.

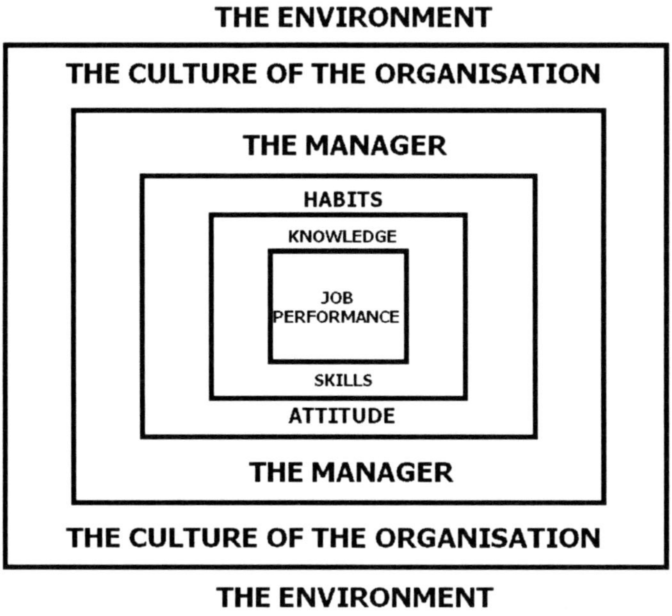

THE ENVIRONMENT

THE CULTURE OF THE ORGANISATION

THE MANAGER

HABITS

KNOWLEDGE

JOB PERFORMANCE

SKILLS

ATTITUDE

THE MANAGER

THE CULTURE OF THE ORGANISATION

THE ENVIRONMENT

Figure 22: Influences on Performance

Edgar Schein[30] defines organisational culture as 'the set of shared, taken-for-granted implicit assumptions that a group holds and that determines how it perceives, thinks about, and reacts to its various environments'.

Of late, organisations have attempted to define themselves based upon what is known as a 'balanced scorecard' – meaning that it is recognised that corporate entities are not set up simply to achieve one thing – profitability – but that its accomplishment of corporate goals and the makeup of its being contains a number of elements. A typical balanced scorecard contains four elements: Business Results,

---

[30] *Administrative Science Quarterly*, June 1996.

Efficiency, Customer Satisfaction, and Organisational Development. The organisation then sets up criteria to measure itself against such a set of scorecard elements in order to determine whether it is achieving their goals.

It is in the area of organisational development that we find such items as:

- Reward for effort.
- Knowledge and skills to carry out a role.
- Learning and development opportunities.
- Management and leadership

The lifeblood of the organisation is the sales function, but is that true of all organisations? The role of sales coach is to improve the performance of the sales team. On the one hand, this appears to be a reasonably clear responsibility but, on the other hand, there are many influences on sales motivational and performance. Those influences also extend to others within the organisation. For example, the sales team may gain a contract to supply a customer – but the warehousing and distribution department might not have enough stock to fulfil the order. The salesperson may have promised a customer an advertising campaign to support a promotion of goods in their stores – but the marketing department budget might be allocated somewhere else. The sales coach may have planned a campaign based upon a certain number of salespeople in their team – but the HR department suddenly freezes recruitment.

Sales coaching is not always just about the sales coach and the salespeople who report to them – sometimes, it can involve circumstances and situations beyond the sales coach's control.

The following is a description of the ideal circumstances required to implement a successful sales coaching culture within an organisation. Whilst I accept that most organisations as yet will not be geared up for this approach, what I can say with confidence is that any watering down of this ideal situation in turn will water down the effectiveness of purpose of sales coaching.

THE ROLE OF THE SALES COACH

Ideally the sales coach should be the line manager. The sales coach should be supported in his/her sales coaching activities by the 'meta coach' (the manager's manager) and if there is one, by the learning and development department (L&D) – which may or may not be out-sourced (**Figure 23**).

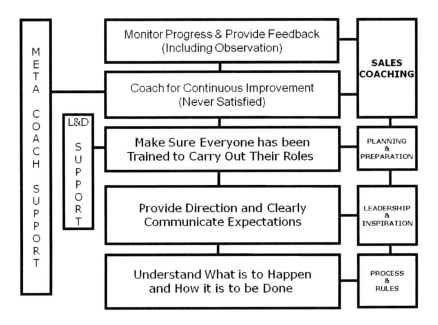

Figure 23: The Role of the Sales Coach

Understand What is to Happen and How it is to be Done - Process & Rules

The sales coach needs a clear understanding of the process and rules attached to a particular sales job. The process is a combination of the job role and accountabilities; the rules are a combination of competencies – behavioural and technical; and the attitude and habits the sales coach wants the job-holder to adopt. Together, these elements form the 'game plan' – this is how we engage customers.

In order to transfer learning from the classroom to the workplace, sales coaches must be involved in a formal follow-up process. Line managers acting as sales coaches should attend at least one session of any sales training programme (if only as observers), so that there is a direct connection between theory and practice. This will help communication significantly and will reduce potential misunderstanding or confusion between sales, sales management, and sales training. In this way, the sales coach becomes the connecting drive-shaft (**Figure 24**) between process definitions (the game plan), training, and what is expected to happen with the customer following training.

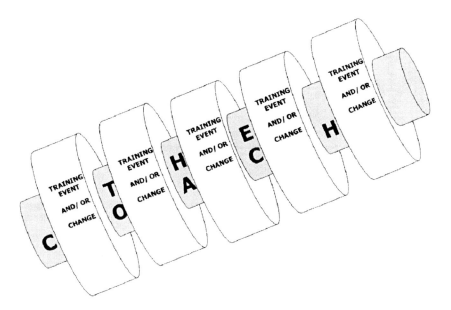

Figure 24: The Sales Coach as Drive-Shaft

Habits for salespeople and for sales coaches can include a range of behaviours primarily outside of customer contact but which ultimately influence customer contact. Part of the briefings for the sales teams and training for the sales coaches should include the self-development of rules.

*Provide Direction & Clearly Communicate Expectations - Leadership
& Inspiration*

The sales coach provides clear leadership and direction by ensuring
that everyone understands what is to be done and to what minimum
standard. The sales coach's first role is to set the scene by ensuring
that everyone understands the game plan and the part they will play
in the success of the team.

Remember, sales coaching is not just a technique – it is a culture.
As such, it is important that sales coaching as an activity is not seen as
a one-off. The sales coach has to demonstrate that sales coaching is
both the current and future mechanism from which current
achievement and future success will emanate. Initially, the new sales
coach has to overcome the tendency of teams to adopt a 'wait and
see' attitude towards something that could be viewed as just another
training initiative – e.g., "I've seen this before. Keep your head down
and, in due course, it will go away and they will move onto
something else". It is critical that the sales coach and other managers
– within the line and beyond – demonstrate longevity in this
initiative. Sales coaching will deliver continuous improvement.
However, it requires continuous commitment, and the active support
of senior management. This latter element is explained in the section
on Meta Coaching.

*Make Sure Everyone has been Trained to Carry out Their Roles -
Planning & Preparation*

The sales coach is supported in providing training to new and
existing sales team members by L&D. Ensuring that people have
been sufficiently trained to carry out their roles to a minimum
standard is an integral element of effective sales coaching. The
experience of non-transference of training from the classroom to the
workplace is common in organisations that do not have a sales
coaching culture. The drive then becomes a demand for more sales
training. Yet more is neither necessarily better nor required. What is
required is a mechanism for moving a training intervention from
theory to reality. The role of the sales coach is vital in this regard.
However, the role of L&D also is significant in the provision of tools
to the sales coach following delivery of a sales training intervention.

In essence, L&D must supply the sales coach with the assessment tools needed to check that knowledge and skills acquisition has been achieved. This provides an important message to everyone attending training courses that a payback is required.

Coach for Continuous Improvement (Never Satisfied) – Sales Coaching

In my discussions with top performers in sports and the performance arts, and in common with successful people in most walks of life, one of the secrets of achievement is never being satisfied with their current performance. As in the Professional Processes model (**Figure 6**), the coach is instrumental in fostering this attitude amongst the team.

Monitor Progress & Provide Feedback (Including Observation) – Sales Coaching

Sales coaching is a hands-on activity. It is interventionist. It is focused on practical solutions for performance improvement requirements. Some sales coaching is off-line but, as with coaching in other professions such as sports and the performing arts, the proof of the results of a sales coach's intervention is seen on the pitch.

Many work-based coaches rely on facts, figures, discussion, records, and anecdotal evidence to monitor progress. The sales coach relies on all of these but additionally checks out those findings by observing the salesperson selling to the customer. The requirement to observe is crucial. The sports coach does not work with the team on Wednesday on the practice pitch and say "You have a game on Saturday. Enjoy it and call me after the match and let me know how you got on". They watch the game from the sidelines. The dance coach does not work with performers during the day and say "You have a performance this evening. Enjoy it and let me know how you got on". They sit in on the performance. Yet many managers discuss with their teams what is supposed to happen in front of customers and then rely on the salesperson to tell them what actually happened. This is why salespeople often provide feedback of this kind to the manager: "I did everything we agreed I should do. I made a really good presentation – but the customer just wasn't interested". The only way to avoid this happening is to observe sales meetings yourself.

THE ROLE OF THE META COACH

A fundamental principle of sales coaching is that it seeks to foster a trait found in all high achievers – namely, a sense of personal responsibility. Personal responsibility is a learned trait. Whereas much of our personality is a result of lessons we learn from parents and guardians in our childhood, our corporate personality is learned from our managers. In the sales programmes I run, the salesperson is taught, and they accept, that the customer's behaviour (in buying or not buying) is a consequence of their (the salesperson's) behaviour. Likewise, I teach new sales coaches that the behaviour of their salespeople (resulting in the customer buying or not buying) is a consequence of the coach's behaviour. There is, therefore, a direct link between all managers in the line and the customer. Everyone in the management line has an influence on both the salesperson and the customer (**Figure 25**). Everyone is in selling.

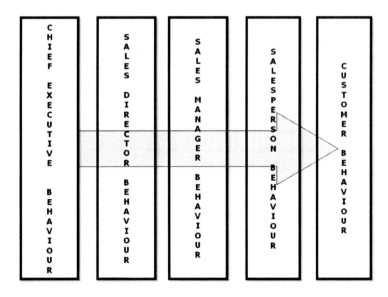

Figure 25: Everyone is in Selling

The key to transferring sales training from the classroom to the workplace is the amount of involvement from the sales manager. However, sales managers are no different to salespeople when it comes to implementing training. Knowledge acquired and skills tried out or merely discussed in the classroom often remain there, as the return to the workplace throws up the same environment as before. Unless someone makes an effort to check what has changed since a training intervention, then nothing will change. Therefore, the person best placed to verify that the newly-learned sales coaching skills are being used by the sales manager is the sales manager's line manager. For this reason, I propose the creation and definition of a Company Coaching Squad, which includes the role of the meta coach. The meta coach is the coach of the coach.

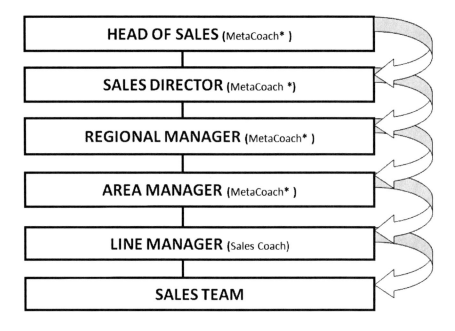

•METACOACH = COACH OF THE COACH

Figure 26: The Company Coaching Squad

It is up to the meta coach to decide the level of involvement they have in hands-on coaching activity. Meta coaching, however, is critical, especially if there is a corporate desire to see change and improvement in sales outputs. The greatest influence on a salesperson is their manager. The greatest influence on the front-line sales manager is his/her manager.

If the company wants this initiative to be successful, and it can be, you need the help of the complete management line acting as meta coaches – yet, that involvement need not be onerous. That said, the more the meta coach undertakes meta coaching with line reports, the quicker the culture will be developed and the greater will be the influence on sales coaching activity. The meta coach is focussed on the processes and rules being employed by their direct report only (**Figure 27**). They do not coach the salesperson.

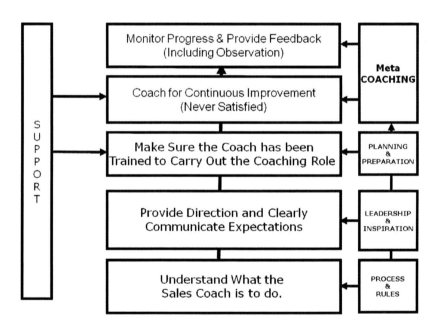

Figure 27: The Meta Coach in Action

The meta coach needs to ensure that the sales coach:
- Displays a significant understanding of the sales coaching process.
- Provides leadership and inspiration for the sales team.

- Monitors the sales team's performance and undertakes regular observations of interactions between the team and customers.
- Undertakes sales coaching sessions with the sales team.
- Displays a 'we get better – we do not stand still' attitude by their behaviour and actions.
- Has the requisite level of skills to perform the role effectively.

From time to time, therefore, the meta coach will need to observe the sales coach. Thus, the meta coach in turn needs to:

- Understand what the sales coach is to do.
- Provide direction and clearly communicate their expectations to the sales coach with regard to the implementation of sales coaching.
- Appraise the ability of the sales coach to carry out this role and elicit assistance if this falls short.
- On field visits, look for evidence of sales coaching activity.

LEARNING AND TIMING

Learning to become a sales coach does not happen overnight. As with acquiring coaching skills in other professions (sports, performing arts, etc), it requires practice, application, and feedback. Unless you already have an audience who are particularly well disposed to sales coaching as an intervention, then the time required from planning to successful implementation may be anything from six to 18 months (**Figure 28**).

That said, I know from experience that there will be an instant lift. The process has a tendency to draw sales managers and salespeople together – focusing on improvement solutions rather than end results. Once coaches begin the process of acquiring basic levels of knowledge and sales coaching skills, some improvement will be seen.

Learning something new that demands the adoption of high-level skills is not just about skills development – it is also about knowledge and attitude (**Figure 29**).

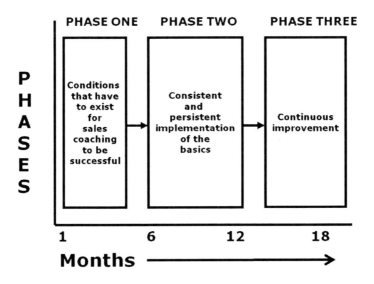

Figure 28: Phases in Becoming a Sales Coach

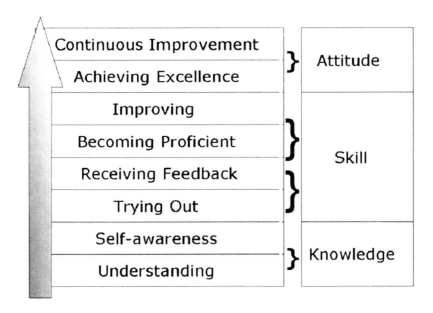

Figure 29: Continuous Improvement is the Aim

Knowledge in this context is about understanding how sales coaching works – and self-awareness about 'where my starting point is and how far have I to go?'. Skills acquisition is about doing – trying out something new and receiving feedback. Then it is about practising until the person becomes proficient and, through further practice, improves their skill. Attitude is about achieving excellence – perhaps even teaching others. The aim is continuous improvement.

It might be said "If you know the answer, why not simply tell people what sales coaching is and how to do it rather than involve them in a protracted process of training?". It is not as simple as that. The difference between giving people the answer, rather than having them come to the conclusion themselves, is grounded in how coaching works in the first place. It is more effective if people come up with this answer themselves by asking them what they think and exploring the answers until they reach the same conclusion – but with a lot more conviction and commitment.

Self-awareness involves self-discovery. People achieve understanding by being involved in the construction of the. Experiential learning is better – because it remains learned.

THE ROLE OF THE TRAINING DEPARTMENT IN A SALES COACHING ENVIRONMENT

Realistic Training Interventions

Ensure that training interventions enable salespeople to acquire the requisite levels of knowledge and skills to meet the minimum requirements of the job role within a realistic time-scale. Acquiring high levels of knowledge and skills does not happen overnight. Lengthy courses, on the other hand, can produce something akin to information overload. What works is the 'whole-part-whole' approach explained earlier (**Figure 10**).

If the acquisition of skill is important, then role-playing should receive a greater allocation of time. It also needs to be borne in mind that unlearning an existing behaviour and replacing it with a new behaviour will require significant repetition, both on the course and following the training event. In turn, this could mean that courses become shorter but more frequent. I accept that this can lead to management frustration and a pressure to run full-day events and cram a training agenda with more rather than less. It rarely works. In skills training, less is more.

Testing

Testing both knowledge and skills levels is good practice, whether in a regulated environment or not. If trainees know that they will be tested on a training event, they tend to prepare better and pay greater attention, especially if the results of testing are published. It is acknowledged that testing will add to administration and take up some training time on an event, but the payback will be worth it.

Sales Coaching Tools

Ensure that the sales coach is provided with the tools to check the expected levels of knowledge and skills acquisitions acquired on a training intervention – in particular:

- Learning outcomes expected.
- Knowledge that should have been acquired, with questions the sales coach can ask and what the answers should be.
- Skills that should have been acquired, with a role-play scenario the sales coach can conduct to check whether those skills are evident.
- A formal feedback system, which the sales coach must make to the training department.

Sales coaches also should assess periodically the competence of the salespeople. Using a formal system not only helps with determining potential training needs but will help the company to provide evidence that those dealing with customers are doing so in a prescribed manner and being monitored.

I have described the role of the meta coach in terms of influencing and monitoring the sales coaching activities being undertaken. I recognise however that gaining support for the meta coaching role can sometimes be akin to, as the saying goes, 'allowing the turkeys to vote for Christmas'. The difficulty of involving senior managers in sales coaching is not new. All I can suggest is that, in the most successful coaching programmes I have instigated, much of the success has been down to senior management embracing by their actions, not just by their words, the coaching ethos required of others.

I recommend that a tracking mechanism is put in place, which the meta coach can ask to see on a regular basis, and which would ensure that sales coaching as an activity is seen as integral to the role, not simply as an adjunct when appropriate or when time is available. Sales managers are notorious for saying that they simply do not have time to coach.[31] This is primarily because many line managers see coaching as an extra activity – not central to their role of staff development.

---

[31] The 2007 CIPD report on coaching again highlights 'time availability' as an issue for managers.

CHAPTER 13

THE COACH IN ACTION

Strive for excellence, not perfection. *H. Jackson Brown Jr.*

This chapter focuses on a number of vignettes taken from actual case studies in which the POWER© coaching model has been used. I have changed the names of the people involved, but the situations are real. They demonstrate how coaching has enhanced performance. Also explained will be the meta coach role – the person who coaches the coach.

VIGNETTE 1: GAINING SALES APPOINTMENTS BY TELEPHONE

Sheila is a life insurance salesperson. She recently attended a sales course where she was taught to use a particular sales script that had been found to be effective. When she started in the field, her appointment rate was very poor, which was put down to her inability to get client appointments by telephone. She was now in danger of not surviving past her probationary period. I had covered the purpose of the session, and what we felt we were able to achieve within the timescale.

Coach: What's the long-term goal from contacting this person?
Sheila: To sell them some life insurance.
Coach: What will stop that from happening?
Sheila: Well, for a start, they might not want to see me.
Coach: Does that happen often?
Sheila: Quite a lot.
Coach: Why is that?
Sheila: I do not know. They just do not want insurance.

Coach:	Is that what you are asking for?
Sheila:	No. I ask for an appointment to see them.
Coach:	So it's the appointment they turn down, is it?
Sheila:	I suppose so.
Coach:	Before we progress, you need to decide what it is that they're objecting to.
Sheila:	I do not know.
Coach:	Are you using the telephone sales script you were given?
Sheila:	Yes.
Coach:	Say it to me.

The performer repeated her version of the script, which turned out not to be the same one she had been supplied with.

Coach:	It's not the same as the one we developed last time.
Sheila:	It did not work.
Coach:	How often did it not work?
Sheila:	I do not know. I tried it a few times and it did not work.
Coach:	So you changed it.
Sheila:	Yes.
Coach:	And what happened?
Sheila:	It still does not work.
Coach:	What do you think the reason is?
Sheila:	They still do not want insurance.
Coach:	Can we go back to the beginning? What is it you want from me?

In some cases, performers can be hostile to change and any implied criticism. It can be frustrating for the coach to be faced with someone who appears to lack any positive intention of learning, but the coach needs to be patient and to focus on his/her coaching performance at this stage, not the reticence of the performer. I pursued the point.

Sheila:	Well, I'm not getting any appointments. I think it's more to do with the fact that business is tight at the moment rather than my style. I've done what you said, but it does not work.

Coach: Just a minute. At the moment, the script you developed does not work. Others using the same script are making it work. Let me hear you say the script we gave you.

The performer repeated her own version. I asked her to say it again three more times.

Coach: It's different every time.
Sheila: Well, it's flexible. It depends on what the prospect says.
Coach: But not only am I the same person listening, I also have not said anything yet.

It took some time but the performer eventually realised that she did not have a script and the request for the appointment depended entirely on how she felt at the time. Considering that getting appointments by telephone is most salespeople's *bête noir*, she usually felt very negative and nervous about making telephone calls — hence the poor response.

Coach: I want you to use the script.

There are times when the coach has to impose a regime. It is pointless allowing people to run the 100 metres in whatever direction they like — they would be disqualified. When you coach a football team, there are rules about the area of play and the time allowed in each half. In some sales situations, and this is the part most salespeople and managers resist, there may be rules, like a script, that have to be enforced. We had already proven, by using this particular scripting method, that the appointment rates for other salespeople had increased dramatically. In some cases, it had helped to move people from a 20 per cent strike rate to 80 per cent within one session. If, as a coach, you have prescribed something that works generally as part of the initial training programme, which was the case here, and people who choose to ignore it have not found a better way of doing it, which again was the situation here, the coach can insist on imposing what was agreed at the training stage before going on.

Coach: I want you to use the script and I'm going to watch you, listen to you, and record your performance.

In this scenario, it became apparent to the performer that her performance was so poor that even those wanting to buy insurance would not give her an appointment. I insisted she keep practising the same script, playing it back to her each time. Each time, it sounded better. Within an hour of adopting the script and having her performance coached, she was achieving high levels of success on the telephone.

VIGNETTE 2: TRAINING THE SALES TRAINER

Peter is a sales training consultant. He writes and delivers training events to all levels of salespeople. Whilst an accomplished writer, his delivery style was very stilted, so much so that the response he used to get from course delegates was less than favourable. I watched his presentations on a number of occasions and, although we found them to be technically accomplished, they lacked something. I noticed that Peter wrote all of his notes out in minute detail prior to delivering a session. During a session, he would have his notes in front of him, meticulously typed up and laid out so that he could see them. As soon as he moved away from his notes, however, he looked and sounded ill-at-ease.

I had a record that, some time ago, I asked him to forget his notes and deliver from slides. It is the style I use myself when delivering training or making speeches at conferences or seminars. I put the slides together first, then write up a script, and then deliver from the slides. The advice had gone unheeded.

Coach: Peter, I've got 30 minutes now. How can we best use the time?

Peter: I'd like you to help me sort out this problem with my delivery. I just cannot get it right.

Coach: In 30 minutes, it might not be possible to do a complete job. Can I suggest that you present your latest session to me? I'll watch it, and record it. We can have a brief discussion, after which I want you to watch the video playback, and tell me what you see.

Peter agreed. We arranged for a couple of people to attend the session. His presentation took 15 minutes, and sure enough, during it, whilst he stayed near his notes, everything went well. As soon as he ventured out of sight of his notes, his presentation became lack-lustre. Another problem was that, even when in sight of his notes, because he kept looking down, the whole presentation lacked impact. After the others had left, we discussed it.

Coach: What did you feel?
Peter: I don't know. It was all right, but it wasn't great.
Coach: What were you trying to do?
Peter: I was attempting to impart some knowledge.
Coach: Anything else?
Peter: I suppose I was trying to motivate people to learn.
Coach: Did you achieve that?
Peter: I don't think so.
Coach: How do you know?
Peter: I did not feel good, and they did not look particularly inspired.

We had been rewinding the tape, and began playing it back with the volume switched off.

Coach: Where did not you feel comfortable?
Peter: What do you mean?
Coach: You say you did not feel good. By that, do you mean comfortable?
Peter: Yes.
Coach: So where wasn't it comfortable?
Peter: I do not know. Do you mean physically?
Coach: Yes.
Peter: I suppose round about here. [He pointed to his shoulder.]
Coach: Look at the playback, and tell me what's happening.

A video can be a very useful tool, especially if used correctly. I find it extremely useful to turn the sound off on playback, as the noise can be distracting. In most cases, what you want to focus on are the body movements. In a case like this, they tell you more about performance than the words that are used.

Peter: I do not look too happy.
Coach: What else?
Peter: I look uncomfortable.
Coach: All the time?
Peter: No, just some of the time.
Coach: When in particular?
Peter: When I'm standing near the desk. And when I return to my desk.
Coach: What about when you move away from the desk?
Peter: It looks all right.
Coach: So what is there about the desk?
Peter: It's where my laptop is, which is connected to the projector.
Coach: So what else is there on the desk?
Peter: My notes are on it. [Peter began to laugh.]
Coach: What are you laughing at?
Peter: You are going to tell me it's the notes. You've told me that before.
Coach: I'm not going to tell you anything. What do you do when you stand at the desk and when you return to the desk?
Peter: I look at my notes.
Coach: And what happens?
Peter: I look unhappy. But I'm not, you see. I'm only studying my notes.
Coach: I understand. But what do you look like?
Peter: Unhappy.
Coach: And what effect is it having on the audience?
Peter: It probably makes them unhappy.
Coach: So what else could you do?
Peter: I could smile.
Coach: What else?
Peter: I could look at them more.

Coach:	What will that mean?
Peter:	I will not be able to do both. I mean, I cannot look at them and my notes at the same time.
Coach:	What else could you do?
Peter:	I could learn my notes. But I might forget something.
Coach:	Will they know?
Peter:	I don't suppose so.
Coach:	When do you look happy?
Peter:	When I'm standing in the front of the table. Except for that part.
Coach:	What happened there?
Peter:	I forgot about something and went back to the table to look at my notes.
Coach:	If you are interested, I could suggest another way of looking at it, but it's up to you if you want to explore it.
Peter:	Yes.
Coach:	Could it be that you did not forget something as much as remembered that your notes were on the table?
[Peter began to laugh again.]	
Coach:	So what do you want to do?
Peter:	I want to try it again without my notes.
Coach:	When?
Peter:	Now.

I asked Peter to do his presentation again a few more times. I left him to record himself, playing it back each time and looking at his performance. I had run out of time, but I did agree that, later on, I would watch him again. By then, he had improved immensely. He is now a very accomplished speaker and continues to improve.

VIGNETTE 3: COACHING MANAGERS: THE ROLE OF THE META COACH

The meta coach is the coach of the coach. Even the coach needs feedback, and similarly the POWER© model can be used to give that internal feedback on the coach's performance. The problem you may face with managers is their reluctance to be coached at coaching. A good way to set this up is to arrange a session which involves a physical activity so that all concerned can 'feel' the effect of being coached, and of being coached as a coach.

One way that works is to take managers to a golf driving range, to arrange for a golf session indoors using a net, or to buy some of those small plastic balls, the size of golf balls, which are hollow and have holes in the sides. These can still be hit quite hard, but they do not inflict any damage when they hit anything. Obviously, if you are going to do this indoors, you will need a large room with enough height to be able to swing a golf club. Place a screen five to 10 yards away, or hang a large sheet from the ceiling. No matter how hard you hit the ball, the sheet or the screen will stop it.

Pick someone who has tried playing golf but is not very good, and find an experienced player to coach them. Explain to the coach that you want them to coach the performer to hit the ball better. You then stand near the coach and, when appropriate, call 'time out' so that you can ask the coach the same coaching questions as are part of the model. The chances are that the experienced golfers will not be able to resist 'telling' people what to do. The effect of you asking the POWER questions will help them realise what it is like to be coached, and what they are doing to the performer.

If the golf set-up is inappropriate, the same exercise can be achieved through playing snooker. Simplify the game by leaving just the cue ball and a few colours.

Coaching sessions and meta coaching sessions then can be arranged. It is possible to go even further by standing another coach next to the meta coach, asking them what they are trying to achieve. Depending on the number of managers available, the meta coach role can be extended infinitely and, at times, can result in an enjoyable, humorous, and yet powerful learning experience. In fact, if you are training in a hotel that has a snooker table, using that also can help in straightforward coaching.

The following case study involves Alex who was a sales manager. He had been on a sales call with Sally, a salesperson who was performing on or around the acceptable performance line. After the call, Alex attempted to coach her to increase her performance next time. When observing the coaching session, it was useful to take some notes.

Coach:	What were you trying to achieve, Alex?
Alex:	I was trying to get Sally to admit that she could have performed better on that last call.
Coach:	Was that your purpose or hers?
Alex:	Mine.
Coach:	So what was her purpose?
Alex:	I don't know.
Coach:	So what's the problem?
Alex:	You'll probably say that she will not be committed to a course of action if she is not involved in setting out her own objectives.
Coach:	OK. Let's go back to the purpose of the coaching session and the observation you made. What's the purpose of a coaching visit?
Alex:	To improve the performance of the salesperson.
Coach:	And how were you to achieve that?
Alex:	By observing Sally on the call and providing her with feedback.
Coach:	Good. What about you? What's the purpose of this session?
Alex:	To help make me a better coach.
Coach:	Is that your objective or mine?
Alex:	Both, I suppose.
Coach:	What will be the effect of making you a better coach?
Alex:	The theory is that my people will perform better.
Coach:	Is it theory or reality?
Alex:	At the moment, it's theory.
Coach:	What's the difference with reality?
Alex:	Well, up to now, it hasn't worked.
Coach:	What hasn't?
Alex:	This coaching thing.
Coach:	What specifically does not work?
Alex:	I've been trying it for a few weeks now, and performance has stayed just the same.
Coach:	So what could you do differently?

Alex: I could go back to doing what I was doing before.

Coach: Which was what?

Alex: Telling people, showing them, motivating them.

Coach: And how was that working?

Alex: All right.

Coach: What levels were people performing at?

Alex: About the same as now.

Coach: So what are you doing differently?

Alex: Coaching them.

Coach: Describe to me specifically what you did on this last session with Sally.

Alex: I got her to tell me what she was doing wrong.

Coach: How did you do that?

Alex: I got her to explain to me what she could have done better.

Coach: So what were you actually saying to her?

Alex: That she could have done something better.

Coach: What in particular did you focus on?

Alex: I asked her what there was about the way she opened the presentation that she could have done better.

Coach: What's the difference between telling her that the opening could have been better, and asking what there was about the opening that could have been better?

Alex: Well, she came up with the answer.

Coach: Alex, what was there about the opening few minutes of your coaching session that could have been handled better, allowing Sally to express herself before you manipulated her into saying that she could have done the opening better?

Alex: Just a minute. Are you saying that I did not coach her properly in the opening few minutes?

Coach: Is that similar to what you did to Sally?

[There was a pause. The penny dropped.]

Coach: Alex, what was the result of this coaching session on Sally's next call?

Alex: It wasn't a great deal better.

Coach: And what have been the results of most of your coaching sessions with others?

Alex: I've already told you, not a lot has changed.

Coach: So what could you do differently?

Alex: OK, so I could try to ask the questions differently.

Coach: What in particular?

Alex: Let them express themselves more.

Coach: What effect would that have?

Alex: You'd say that it would commit them to change if they came up with it in the first place.

Coach: Let's say it actually had that effect, how would that make you feel?

Alex: I'd be happy if they improved.

Coach: What are you feeling at the moment?

Alex: Frustrated.

Coach: What about?

Alex: Well, I know what to say. It's just that ...

Coach: Just what?

Alex: Sometimes, it just does not come out right.

Coach: So what could you do about it?

Alex: Practise it more.

Coach: What support do you need?

Alex: I'd appreciate it if you continued to give me some feedback.

It took a few more sessions before Alex grasped the fact that he was manipulating responses, not empowering people. We reconvened.

Coach: Alex, let's have another look at the purpose of the coaching session with Sally. You said that the purpose of a coaching visit is to improve the performance of a salesperson. Does it matter how that improvement happens?

Alex: No, I suppose not.

Coach: Does it matter?

Alex: Only if she does something wrong that contravenes the rules.

Coach: And, in that case, what would you do?

Alex: I'd set out at the beginning what the rules were and how the game had to be played.

Coach: OK. So in the case of Sally, does she break the rules?

Alex: No.

Coach: So, as she's not exactly performing below the acceptable performance line, does it matter where the improvement comes from?

Alex: No.

Coach: Does this stop you from dictating the purpose of the coaching session?

Alex: No, I suppose not. The purpose for me remains to improve her performance.

Coach: And how often do you set this out as a general aim of your role as a coach?

Alex: I take it as read.

Coach: What else could you do?

Alex: I could talk about it more when I'm out with people.

Coach: Would that help?

Alex: It certainly wouldn't do any harm.

Coach: When else could you do it?

Alex: At sales meetings?

Coach: So when will you do that?

I agreed that Alex would revisit his vision at the next sales meeting and that we would observe him doing so and provide him with feedback. This coaching session resulted in Alex proposing that he might be manipulating people into providing him with the answers he wanted. He agreed to role-play having his salespeople set their own objectives, which was done until he sounded and appeared convincing.

Within three months of this event, Alex had conducted another three coaching sessions and observations with Sally. The feedback from her was extremely positive and she became one of Alex's team who regularly exceeded target, providing Alex with the space he needed to improve the others in his team.

VIGNETTE 4: TRAINING COMES BEFORE COACHING

I have presented extracts above on some coaching scenarios. Let's look briefly at two final case studies.

In the first case, a bank was concerned with the low customer take-up of serious illness cover by customers taking out mortgages. Following a training needs analysis with the loan advisors who sold the products, it became apparent that there were both training issues and coaching requirements.

Before looking at coaching, it was necessary in the first instance to address the training area. The training issues revolved around a lack of knowledge of the serious illness product. To help address these needs, a training video was developed with successful salespeople describing the product features and benefits, together with simulated sales interviews with customers in which the product was successfully sold.

Training sessions were held using the sales training video, together with some prepared sales scripts. Following the course, which involved sales role-plays, all loan advisors had specific action plans that they undertook to complete back on the job. Their sales managers undertook to sign off the loan advisors as competent when they satisfactorily role-played customer interviews using serious illness cover. When advisors were signed off as being able to demonstrate that they had reached an acceptable level of performance and started selling serious illness cover, the sales figures improved. However, the exercise also had highlighted that some advisors sold significantly more product than others. This is where coaching played its part.

Regional sales managers undertook to work with the loan advisors over a four-month period with the express purpose of developing their performance to higher levels beyond that reached by the training initiative. They followed the POWER© coaching model with the advisors. Following each coaching visit, the POWER form (**Appendix 2**) was completed and copies made. Improving performance was the agreed focus.

Some very positive results were evident, including increased results of 20 per cent. The feedback from customers was positive, as they bought relevant products that addressed their security needs when taking out mortgages. Reflecting on the success, one regional sales manager commented: "I always knew my sales staff had the potential to sell more products, but it was only by working in partnership with them, observing them in interviews, and by following a structured coaching approach that their confidence and competence grew".

VIGNETTE 5: MANAGING A PERFORMANCE PROBLEM

When faced with a gap in work performance, some sales managers automatically look for the salesperson to attend a training course. However, deeper analysis is required to discover the issue underlying the poor performance. It might be lack of training, but there might be some other cause.

The case study below highlights some of the areas that need to be looked at first where there is a performance gap, before coaching is introduced. It also represents a useful checklist of questions to ask when confronted with a performance problem.

In this case, the sales manager was concerned that a certain salesperson was behind target and was not converting customer interviews into sales. She sought advice from me before sitting down with the salesperson. I went through the following checklist with her with regard to the performance gap. I sought answers to the following questions:

- Is the salesperson aware that there is a performance gap? (If not, make them aware of the gap.)
- Does the person have the necessary knowledge and skills to do the job? (If not, provide appropriate training.)
- If the person has the knowledge and skills, have they done the job frequently? (If not, provide them with the opportunities to undertake the role more regularly, as their skills might be rusty.)

In this instance, the sales manager confirmed that the salesperson knew that there was a performance gap and that he had been well trained in both the classroom and on the job. I concluded from my assessment that it was not a training issue. I continued with the list of questions, trying to diagnose the full extent of the problem before offering a solution.

- Is the salesperson aware of the standards of performance required to successfully carry out the job?
- Does the salesperson understand the manager's expectations? If so, is he receiving regular feedback on his performance?
- Are the consequences of his performance clear?

If the answer to these questions is 'No', these issues must be addressed in the first instance. For example, the salesperson must be made aware of the benefits of good performance or the consequences of underperformance.

Next:

- Are there any obstacles that stand in the way of good performance? (If there are any barriers to performance, such as lack of resources, authority, or time, these must be addressed and overcome.)

In this case study, following a discussion with the sales manager using this checklist of questions, it became apparent that the salesperson was not getting regular feedback from his sales manager on his interview performance. Furthermore, the sales manager agreed that she did not have enough detail with regard to how the sales interviews were conducted by the salesperson. She could not put her finger on what the person was or was not doing that prevented more sales. There was only one solution: the sales manager had to spend time with the advisor in customer interviews to see exactly what was going wrong. She agreed to start coaching the salesperson over a two-month time-frame and agreed a specific date and time to sit in and observe the next sales interview. The sales manager explained to the salesperson that they would follow the POWER© coaching model.

Over the ensuing two months, the sales manager coached the salesperson. She pinpointed with the performer that, in the interview, although he asked some needs-based questions of customers, he did not feel comfortable or confident asking the customer for the business.

Following this coaching intervention by the sales manager, the salesperson worked hard on the agreed development action points and became stronger when closing the sale. Results improved and the performance gap was closed. The sales manager was very pleased with the enhanced performance. She reinforced the more assertive sales behaviour displayed by the performer by praising them after observing them in action with customers.

The sales manager confided to me that, in the past, she would not have tolerated sub-standard performance for any length of time and would have dismissed the salesperson. This new managerial approach of coaching had worked and she intended to embrace it in her future dealings with her sales team. While she did not believe that it would work in every instance of poor salesmanship, it certainly was a better approach than the traditional management style she had previously used.

CHAPTER 14

EPILOGUE

The opponent inside one's head is more formidable than the one on the other side of the net. Tim Gallwey

It has been said that to stop learning is to stop living. Often, I am asked if I can recommend something to read for people interested in sales coaching. My feeling on this is that you should read anything and everything you can find on the subject. Even if, after reading a complete book or article, you gauge that there was nothing new or you did not particular enjoy it, it is still worth the effort. People spend a great deal more time and energy feeding their bodies than their minds. Some people stretch their bodies to the limit in a vain attempt to stay young or healthy, and yet hardly ever consider how to keep their minds staying young and healthy. Just because you are trying to be a sales coach — and many of the analogies I use come from the athletics world — it does not mean that you have to also end up being a prime contender for a gold medal in the marathon. All things in moderation. However, your mental health ultimately will give you a great deal more pleasure and reward than the health of your body. The maxim 'a healthy mind in a healthy body' is all a matter of intensity. People have a tendency to vacillate towards a particular area of interest and, at times, keeping physically fit and keeping mentally fit seem to be polarised. Given the choice, I would probably choose the latter. If you can achieve a balance, so much the better, but if time is at a premium, and for most of us it is, then keep your mind alive. If you are driving a car, you need petrol to keep it going. Similarly, your mind drives you on and it needs fuel. Learning is to the mind what fuel is to the car.

The thing about study is that, even if you do not appear to be taking it in, in it goes. The brain has an awesome capacity for recording information. Some communication experts may tell you that items that go into our short-term memory are eventually discarded. Only those that we store in our long-term memory can be recalled. When things happen, we do not make conscious decisions to put the experience in our short-term or long-term memory. Sometimes we remember them, sometimes we do not. It is not memory that is the problem; it is recall. If we knew how, we could recall everything that has ever happened to us. Everything we have ever said, done, or seen is recorded; the problem is that we sometimes lose the key to retrieve it. There are people who develop incredible recall processes, and I do not doubt that, given the correct coaching, we could all learn how to do it. In the meantime, why take the chance that you might miss something? Like me, from time to time you will have remembered something, but not where it came from. It came from a time when you read it, saw it or experienced it. If you fail to keep those experiences going, then you run the risk of closing down your ability to develop new ideas and new approaches.

If you can, put your studies on a formal footing. Take a prescribed course of study. If you already have a degree, take another one. The formality of academic study, at whatever level, can help maintain your impetus for self-improvement.

In terms of the job that we do, then the only recommendation I can make is that you focus on communication. It is communication that shapes the world. Stephen Hawking said:

> Man's greatest achievements have come about through talking.
> Man's greatest failures have come about through not talking.

It is a fact that the increase in communication over the last century paradoxically has reduced our ability to talk to each other. Part of this has to be that information is so readily available in visual form that people have lost the ability to find out things for themselves. Yet the volume of information available in written form is far greater than anything you will see on video or television.

VISION, VISUALISATION, SELF-ESTEEM AND SELF-TALK

What is it that draws you to a particular person? There are people who appear to attract followers, and yet why it happens remains a mystery. They appear to exude a confidence that is difficult to quantify but which has an effect on people they come into contact with. There are leaders who produce in their followers a sense of mission, of belonging, and a desire for achievement based on the needs for intrinsic reward. These people give reference to the achievements of the past, postulate a vision of the future, and influence action in the here and now. Charismatic leaders have vision. They seem to have the ability to get us to actually see the success of the future. They are few and far between.

In discussion with people who have achieved success in one form or another, a recurring theme has been the subject of visualisation. People who are successful or who achieve something see it as a natural extension of their planning process. Success rarely comes as a surprise to the successful. They are geared up for it. They saw it some time ago and told themselves it would happen. It's an old conundrum: are people confident because they are successful, or are people successful because they are confident? Where does confidence come from? Some people will say it comes from within. If that's true, then we all have it. Perhaps some just hide it better than others. The Catch-22 of confidence is that it comes from other people who believe you are confident because you act confidently. It has to do with the conversations you have with yourself — your self-esteem.

People who have great self-esteem regularly tell themselves that they are on the journey to achieving their goals, and that they will succeed. In developing your coaching relationships with your salespeople, you will become a role model for their aspirations, not in terms of their personal goals but in the manner in which they approach it. Whilst motivation is a personal thing, your salespeople will be looking to you for inspiration. You can supply it by showing them how to feel confident in their own abilities. You do this by showing them how confident you are in your own. The feeling of your own self-worth is the single most important winning quality you can possess. It does not simply involve pride in what you have achieved, or even in what you intend to achieve, but a real joy in accepting who you are right now.

The biggest problem many people face is that they have no vision of the future. Your job is helping people develop that vision by expressing your own. The main reasons why people do not achieve their goals is that most are not written down, and very few are verbally expressed. If you have a goal, write it down, and if you want your salespeople to achieve their goals, get them to write theirs down as well. In the process of writing down a goal, it becomes evident that a goal statement alone is worthless. To achieve a goal, you have to know where you are now, where you want to be, and work out how to get there. Most people never write their goals down and, as a consequence, never begin the journey.

As a sales coach, you should keep and regularly update your own personal development plan. What are you trying to achieve as a sales coach? What knowledge, skills and behaviours do you need to adopt, and what level are you currently at? It will soon become apparent that you also need a coach, so get one. If you expect to sell the idea of coaching to others, then they will look to you for an example. If you demonstrate that you believe you know it all and do not need a coach, then they will assume the same of themselves.

Last, get into the habit of seeing yourself achieve, and help your salespeople to see themselves achieving. It involves nothing simpler than closing your eyes and seeing yourself delivering your best performance. Play the scene through in your mind until you can see, hear, feel and even smell the successful performance. If something goes wrong during this scene-setting, rewind and put it right until you see yourself delivering the perfect performance you want. Then repeat it as often as time allows before delivering the performance in reality. It is at this stage that fantasy and reality merge. The scene you have played through in your mind can, and will, happen.

WORDS OF WARNING

As a sales coach, your effect on the performance of others can be dramatic. You could be the catalyst for immense change and for feelings of self-worth and achievement not previously experienced by the people you coach. It is at this stage that the relationship you build of support and trust can become a crutch which, when you try to remove it, results in a collapse of performance and of self-confidence. At all times, you must ensure that people understand that their increase in performance has come from them and not from you. You are a facilitator, but you are not the reason for their newfound success, even though you are key. Unless you develop in them a sense of their responsibility for performance and of their ability to sustain and improve that performance, then you could end up having to support them for life, and that just cannot work.

Avoid trying to change people's personal lives. I know that your personal life can have an effect on your work performance, but that's a matter for people to resolve themselves, not for you as a coach to become enmeshed in. If you become involved in helping them to resolve personal issues, you will cross the boundary between a work coach and a personal counsellor and *confidante*. That is not to say that people will not want to see you as such and will attempt to share their personal problems, but where you can, avoid it. Coaching can be a draining experience, and therefore you need to focus on what you can and cannot reasonably achieve. That is not to say that coaching techniques cannot help people resolve their personal difficulties; it is just that, as an organisational coach, you cannot be all things to all people. The biggest problem you will have is that, in experiencing the power of coaching, in sensing your complicity in the achievement of others, and in the satisfaction of your own personal achievement, you also will be susceptible to believing that in some way all things are possible.

Your job is to give others the confidence to believe in their own ability to solve their own problems without you. Their confidence will come from the realisation that they have the ability to carry out a particular task you give them or that they have previously been unsuccessful at accomplishing. You need to give them a battle they can win, so that they will go on to win bigger battles. Start with things they can do, before giving them tasks they believe they cannot accomplish. Your people may be disappointed if they fail along the way, but remember, in many cases, they will stagnate or atrophy if they do not try.

Their confidence will come from their individual ability to do what is asked of them in their current roles, and this means high-quality induction training. Most people fail in new jobs not because they have not got the ability, but because the induction training was lacking in sufficient direction and initial instruction about what was expected and how to do it. Make sure that, before you begin coaching someone to increased performance, they have received enough initial training.

Their confidence will come from others around them. Your job is to give the team a vision of collective achievement. Confidence comes from the fact that mistakes are tolerated. The best people you have will test the boundaries of your tolerance, and the tolerance of your company.

CONCLUSION

Is sales coaching the answer we have all been looking for? I do not know. What I do know is that it is a better way to manage and to develop salespeople than any other form of development I have yet seen or experienced. Yet if we are also to practise what we preach, then we should keep an open mind to the possibility of something else being developed that can be of use. In the meantime, I am convinced from experience that, by adopting the process contained in this book, you too will experience the powerful effect of POWER© coaching.

APPENDIX 1
THE CHAMPIONS' JOURNAL

The Champion's Journal is intended to be your personal log for the training and development that you undertake during your career. This journal also allows you to record activities or achievements that you take pride in and which are important to you in reaching your own personal goals and ambitions. The sections of the journal can be used to record incidents where you felt you learned something that was important to you. This journal is yours to keep. You must choose whether it is important and valid for you to check where you are going in terms of your performance. It is worth remembering that, if you do not write your goals down, how can you check that they remain what you want? Equally, if you do not log your successes, the development needs you have and the positive changes that will result, how can you be positive that you have achieved them? Sometimes, it can be comforting to be able to remind ourselves of our ability to achieve and our willingness to learn through looking back at the written word.

Development   _____

Date   _____

What was it about?

What did I learn?

How can I apply this to my job?

Further development I should undertake:

APPENDIX 2
THE POWER FORM

This is a permanent record of either an observation or a meeting. Copies should be given to the salesperson to keep and produce at each subsequent meeting. You should complete this immediately after each coaching session.

Salesperson	Location	Sales Coach	Date
(P) What is the purpose of this observation/meeting for the coach?			
(O) What objective(s) is the salesperson hoping to achieve?			
(W) What is the current situation/what happened during the observation/what was discussed?			
(E) What action/step/improvement does the salesperson have to take? What assistance will the coach provide?			
(R) When will this be reviewed?			

RECOMMENDED READING

Adair, John, *Inspirational Leadership,* Institute of Commercial Management, Thorogood, 2002.

Bolt, Peter, *Coaching for Growth*, Oak Tree Press, 2000.

Dick, Frank, 'Fitness to Win', *Target — Management Development Review*, Vol. 4, No. 3, MCB University Press, 1991.

Fournies, Ferdinand, *Coaching for Improved Work Performance*, McGraw Hill, 2000.

Gallwey, Timothy, *The Inner Game of Tennis*, Random House, 1975.

Gladwell, Malcolm, *Outliers: The Story of Success*, Allen Lane, 2008.

Hemery MBE, David, *Sporting Excellence: What Makes a Champion?* Collins Willow, 1991.

Salisbury, Frank, *Sales Training, Second edition*, Gower, 1992.

Salisbury, Frank, *Developing Managers as Coaches*, McGraw-Hill, 1996.

Shenk, David, *The Genius in All of Us*, Icon Books, 2011.

Whitmore, John, *Coaching for Performance*, Nicholas Brearley, 1992.

ABOUT THE AUTHOR

Frank Salisbury is Chairman of the Business & Training Solutions International Group, the Institute of Commercial Management Chief Examiner for Sales & Marketing, and Joint Founder of the Institute of Professional Selling and the International College of Professional Selling. Frank is a leading expert on the subject of Sales, Sales Leadership, and Sales Coaching.

He has designed and delivered a significant range of personal development programmes for individuals and organisations aimed at helping salespeople achieve their potential. These programmes, and this book, have drawn on Frank's research into performance improvement processes in sports, music, acting and dance, and how these could be applied in the world of sales.

He has spoken at numerous sales conferences and seminars where his style has received acclaim from those who hear him speak with a passion for life and achievement.

Frank lives in the North East of England with his wife Pauline. He is a life-long fan of Newcastle United, who he says he has supported through thin and thin.

Previous books by Frank Salisbury include:

- *Coaching Champions: How to Get the Best Out of Your Salespeople*, Oak Tree Press, Dublin, 2001, co-authored with Karl O'Connor and Cariona Neary.
- *Sales Training*: Second Edition, Gower, 1998 (seen as the 'bible' for sales trainers).
- *Developing Managers as Coaches*, McGraw-Hill, 1996.
- *Sales Training*, McGraw-Hill, 1992.

OAK TREE PRESS

Oak Tree Press develops and delivers information, advice and resources for entrepreneurs and managers. It is Ireland's leading business book publisher, with an unrivalled reputation for quality titles across business, management, HR, law, marketing and enterprise topics.

In addition, through its founder and managing director, Brian O'Kane, Oak Tree Press occupies a unique position in start-up and small business support in Ireland through its standard-setting titles, as well training courses, mentoring and advisory services.

Oak Tree Press is comfortable across a range of communication media – print, web and training, focusing always on the effective communication of business information.

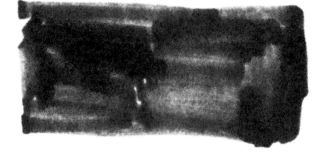

Lightning Source UK Ltd.
Milton Keynes UK
UKOW021153091211

183477UK00001B/11/P